Influenced from Above

Where Faith and
Influence Meet

BRIAN AHEARN
CPT, CMCT

Copyright © 2025 Brian Ahearn

All Rights Reserved. This book or parts thereof may not be reproduced in any form, stored in any retrieval system, or transmitted in any form by any means—electronic, mechanical, photocopy, recording, or otherwise—without prior written permission of the publisher, except as provided by United States of America copyright law.

Scripture quotations taken from the New American Standard Bible® (NASB®), Copyright © 1960, 1971, 1977, 1995, 2020 by the Lockman Foundation. All rights reserved. Used by permission. lockman.org

Printed in the United States of America

ISBN (paperback): 978-1-7331785-6-3
ISBN (ebook): 978-1-7331785-7-0

Contents

Endorsements v
Acknowledgments ix
How to Get the Most Out of This Book xi
Preface xv

Chapter 1 – What Now? 1
Chapter 2 – A Vision 6
Chapter 3 – Laying Out His Fleece 12
Chapter 4 – Responding to the Call 18
Chapter 5 – Where is God? 24
Chapter 6 – Biblical Influence 30
Chapter 7 – Jonathan and David 36
Chapter 8 – Rebuilding the Walls 42
Chapter 9 – Don't Hinder the Children 48
Chapter 10 – Trouble Brewing 54
Chapter 11 – An Influential Article 60
Chapter 12 – Before the Judges 65
Chapter 13 – Martha, Martha 71
Chapter 14 – An Inspired Idea 77
Chapter 15 – The Opposition's Next Move 83
Chapter 16 – A Gentle Answer 89
Chapter 17 – Winning Hearts, Not Just Minds 96
Chapter 18 – From the Mountain Top to the Wilderness 102
Chapter 19 – Speaking the Truth in Love 108

Chapter 20 – Waiting on the Lord 114
Chapter 21 – Anointed for Leadership 120
Chapter 22 – Influence Starts with Connection 126
Chapter 23 – Sowing and Reaping 132
Chapter 24 – A Revelation...138
Chapter 25 – Doubt to Clarity 144
Chapter 26 – A Good Deed? 150
Chapter 27 – Don't be Anxious 156
Chapter 28 – Three Days of Doubt 162
Chapter 29 – A Surprising Ally 167
Chapter 30 – The Prodigal Returns..171

A Deeper Exploration of the Faith–Influence Connection 175
Characters in Order of Appearance 195
About the Author 201

Endorsements

"With this book, Brian Ahearn provides a marriage of spiritual inspiration and psychological illumination that is matchless in my experience."

—Robert B. Cialdini, PhD, author of NYT best sellers, *Influence* and *Pre-Suasion*

"*Influenced from Above* presents a wonderful intersection between science and faith and dispels the common notion that they are at odds. These two domains can actually enrich one another, and this book brings that to life. Brian Ahearn masterfully weaves an inspirational story with the interplay of spiritual beliefs and behavioral science applied ethically and lovingly—making it a compelling read for anyone interested in both personal growth and ethical leadership. However, the real gem lies in the reflection questions that may open a door in your heart."

—Adrian Chong, Principal Consultant & Organizational Psychologist at EREVNA Leadership Asia and a platform speaker at the national Christ at Work Conference

"In our desire not to appear inauthentic or deceptive, Christian Leaders have avoided the topics of Influence and Persuasion and missed opportunities to inspire people for good. As a former pastor turned corporate trainer, I understand the influence challenges in both the Church and corporate settings. Brian is not only a master of influence, but also a faithful follower of Jesus, and shares Dr. Cialdini's 7 Principles of

Persuasion through a story that is captivating, relevant, and desperately needed. This book is one of a kind that every pastor and Christian business leader should own."

—Wes Bryant, founder Commission Sales Coach, former Director of Sports & Recreation Ministry at Greenwood Christian Church and Southport Presbyterian Church

"I've seen how powerful these principles are. Brian's book shows they're not just psychologically true—they're spiritually grounded. A thoughtful guide for anyone who wants to influence with integrity."

—Tommy Schaff, Founder, Major League Sales, Cialdini Method Certified Trainer

"Insightful, inspirational, and most relevant. In Influenced From Above, Brian Ahearn has stepped into the world of other classic narratives (for example, Who Moved My Cheese and The Greatest Salesman in the World). The author tells a heartwarming story while distilling timeless principles that have been used by truly influential leaders for generations. Whether you're in a local church setting or the marketplace, Influenced From Above is relevant to help you be a person of influence with honesty, transparency, and humility."

—Les Hughes, Pastor, Author, Ghostwriter

"My friend Brian Ahearn's new book, Influenced from Above, had me completely captivated—I couldn't stop turning the pages, eager to see what would happen next! Woven into this gripping story is a powerful message: we can all grow our influence through simple, practical skills. Brian not only shows how these "Influence Skills" can be developed, but also highlights how they're modeled throughout Scripture. I used to think being a person of influence simply meant being a good person who keeps their word. But it was through Brian that I discovered influence is a skill we can all intentionally strengthen. Thank you, Brian, for this eye-opening and inspiring read!"

—Bob Tiede, CEO of Leading with Questions
and author of *Leading with Questions*

"I've had the honor of listening to and discussing the concepts of ethical influence with Brian Ahearn numerous times. With each keynote, podcast, or discussion his passion and conviction come through as he offers deep insights for helping all of us work through so many of our everyday situations. In his newest work, *Influenced from Above*, Ahearn puts his wonderful story-telling talents on full display as he shares the fictional journey of community and follows a retired CEO who is called to bring his experiences and his faith to help a local church as it endeavors to take on a monumental community project.

Ahearn does a masterful job exploring how the principles of ethical influence can and do affect our ability every day. In *Influenced from Above*, he goes even deeper as he makes very meaningful faith-based support to already established principles that help guide the characters though their work and conviction to bring their project to fruition.

Regardless of one's spiritual beliefs or affiliations, Brian Ahearn once again shows us (and educates us) that we all have the capabilities to ethically engage with others as we look to affect meaningful change in our lives and communities."

—Chris Cline, author of *The Inertia of Legacy*

Acknowledgments

This book is a sequel to *The Influencer: Secrets to Success and Happiness*, a business parable I wrote several years ago to teach readers about the science of influence (a.k.a. the psychology of persuasion) through storytelling. That book ended with the lead character, John Andrews, stepping away from his corporate career in his early 50s. When I concluded the book, I knew there was more to be written because John still had a whole life ahead of him. But I needed inspiration, a theme to weave throughout the next book. Thankfully, I got that from my daughter.

Writing a book isn't a lone wolf thing, at least not for me. I don't go off to nature, or anywhere else, to be alone with my thoughts and write. I think that would drive me crazy. Instead, throughout the writing process I lean on quite a few people in many ways, so I'd like to acknowledge them for their help and support.

First is my daughter, **Abigail Ahearn**. Many years ago, Abigail came to a presentation I gave in my hometown, Columbus, Ohio. It had been about 10 years since she'd seen me present, so I was curious to know what she thought about the presentation. I got that opportunity the following day over lunch. During our conversation she asked a question that not only stuck with me, but it became the genesis for this book. Regarding the influence coaching and training I do for a living, she asked, "What I want to know is; where is God in all of this?" That led to an interesting exchange, and it sparked my thoughts about the book you're holding in your hands. Thank you, Abigail!

Next is my wife, **Jane Ahearn**. She reads and listens to my books many times as I'm working on them. A naturally curious person, Jane asks insightful questions that cause me to reflect and think more deeply. Her insights were especially appreciated with this project because of her familiarity with my influence training, my previous books, her knowledge of the scriptures, and most of all, her love for the Lord.

Barbara Grassey, my book coach, helped me with each of my influence books. Her guidance on each helped me immensely. It's one thing to write a book but getting it out to the world was something I knew nothing about. Are you considering writing a book? If so, work with Barbara!

Robert Cialdini has been a good friend and mentor for more than 20 years. Our chance encounter because of an email I sent to Stanford in 2003 changed my life. After reading a rough draft he wrote, "And most importantly, it's unique. I've never seen anything like it. The subtitle, 'Where Faith and Influence Meet,' perfectly depicts that uniqueness and foretells a marriage of spiritual inspiration with psychological illumination that is matchless in my experience." Wow! I could not have received higher praise. Thank you, Bob.

How to Get the Most Out of This Book

Whether you picked up this book because you're a fan of Robert Cialdini, a person of faith, or someone who simply wants to be more intentional about how you influence others, I want you to get the most out of this experience. That's why I've included a reflection at the end of every chapter. These aren't throwaway prompts. They're invitations—to slow down, think deeply, and begin connecting influence and faith in ways you might not have before. Below are suggestions to help you go deeper.

1. Begin with a Moment of Silence
Before you read each chapter, take a minute to pause. You might whisper a short prayer, "Lord, show me what you want me to take away from what I'm about to read." That simple act of intention can make a big difference in what sticks with you.

2. Journal Your Thoughts
Have a notebook or journal nearby, or just write on the book pages. After reading a chapter and reflecting, write down your thoughts. There's something powerful about putting pen to paper. It helps clarify thinking and makes it easier to recognize patterns in how God is shaping your influence.

3. Read It with Others
This book is meant to be shared. It works well in:

- Book clubs
- Small groups at church
- Mentorship settings
- Christian business networking groups

Discussing the material with others opens the door to deeper insight and real-life application. You may be surprised how someone else's perspective draws out something you missed.

4. Let Each Chapter Settle
It might be tempting to fly through this in a few sittings—but don't. Each chapter builds on the last, and each reflection question is a nudge toward something God might be trying to show you. Take your time. Influence is a skill, and it's not developed in a day.

5. Look for the Connection
You'll notice Cialdini's principles of influence woven into the narrative, but the deeper layer is how those principles intersect with timeless Biblical truths. Ask yourself:
"Where do I see Jesus living this principle?"
"How does this align—or clash—with how I've been using influence?"
"What needs to change in me?"

6. Practice What You're Learning
This isn't a theory book. It's meant to be lived. Try applying one idea from each chapter in your conversations, leadership, or personal life. The more you practice, the more naturally these ideas will become part of how you show up in the world.

7. Share Your Story
If something in this book impacts you, don't keep it to yourself. Share it with a friend, on social media, or with your team. When you tell your story, you multiply your influence and encourage others to think differently, too.

8. Revisit Often
You'll likely find new insights each time you return to this book. Influence, like faith, is a journey. What resonates with you today might hit differently six months—or six years—from now.

Preface

"What I want to know is: where is God in all this?"

—Abigail Ahearn

My daughter's question over lunch in July 2019 stopped me in my tracks. The day before, I'd given a presentation on Robert Cialdini's principles of influence, a topic I had studied and taught for years, and Abigail was in the audience. Her question made me realize—I had never seriously considered where faith fits into the influence equation.

As we sat outside a Mexican restaurant on a beautiful summer day, her question ignited a conversation and sparked a burning desire within me to explore the question of how faith and influence intersect.

As we spoke, some connections became obvious: The Lord's call to "Do unto others as you'd have them do unto you" was a clear application of reciprocity.

Others weren't so clear, at least on the surface. For example, I told Abigail about the principle of liking, that it's easier for people to say "yes" to you if they like you. Everyone gets that because it seems like common sense. But most people miss this key element; it's more about you liking the people you're with than it is trying to get them to like you. That subtle difference? It changes everything.

I recall telling her, "I can't necessarily talk about love in a corporate setting but if people use this principle the right way, it gets them pretty close to love. Why? Because we naturally want what's best for people we consider friends, often placing their wellbeing above our own. When they know we truly care for them, they become much more open to whatever we might ask or propose."

In the years since that conversation, I began to think more and more about how the principles of influence had a connection to faith. I've not come across any resource that blends those topics, so I set out to change that. The more I explored, the more I realized something profound—these principles weren't just useful strategies for persuasion; they were fundamental truths about human nature. And if they reflect something deeper within us, might they point to something—or Someone—greater?

The answer, I believe, is God. He designed us to respond to certain psychological and relational cues because they reflect deeper spiritual realities. And that's where science comes in. Some see a conflict between science and faith, but I see confirmation. The more I study influence, the more clearly I see science confirming what Scripture has proclaimed for centuries. In fact, it excites me when I discover how Biblical principles are supported by findings from science. Here's one example:

Jesus told his followers, "You cannot serve God and mammon (money)." In *Sway: The Irresistible Pull of Irrational Behavior*, Ori Brafman and Rom Brafman share results from brain imaging studies. They write, "Unlike, say, the parts of our brain that control movement and speech, the pleasure center and the altruistic center cannot both function at the same time; either one or the other is in control" (p. 141). They go on, "It's as if we have two 'engines' running our brains that can't operate simultaneously. We can approach a task either altruistically or from a self-interested perspective" (p. 142). Isn't it fascinating that Jesus's words from 2,000 years ago are being validated by modern brain science?

The principles of influence are validated by science too. Social psychologists and behavioral economists create rigorously controlled experiments designed to find out how people respond in different situations. Of course, not everyone responds exactly the same, but with large enough samples, we see consistent patterns in how people respond to different influence approaches.

Preface

In 2021, I released my third book, *The Influencer: Secrets to Success and Happiness*. It's a business parable designed to teach readers about the principles of influence in a story format. It follows John Andrews, an ordinary person who—through mentors, coaches, and real-life experiences—becomes an extraordinary influencer.

The more I thought about influence, faith, and *The Influencer*, I saw an opportunity to address the faith and influence connection in a similar story approach with John Andrews in his next phase of life. Unlike *The Influencer*, which focused primarily on influence in business, *Influenced from Above* continues John's journey, but this time it's not just about worldly success—it's about eternal significance.

Influence and persuasion are often taboo subjects within the church community. Why? Because each is incorrectly associated with manipulation. Not wanting to appear as if we're deceiving people into believing our message, or to come off as inauthentic, we avoid the topics altogether. That's unfortunate because when we don't consider how to influence people ethically, it hinders the opportunities for others to consider our message, which could make a lasting impact in their lives and ultimately bring more good into the world.

I mentioned faith and science earlier. I hope by reading this book, you'll see that the two don't have to be in opposition. I invite you to explore the principles of influence with me—not just as tools for success and happiness, but also as a way to live out your faith boldly, influence others for good, and leave an eternal impact.

—Brian Ahearn

Chapter 1 – What Now?

"'For I know the plans that I have for you,' declares the Lord, 'plans for welfare and not for calamity to give you a future and a hope.'"

—Jeremiah 29:11

The sky was clear, and it was getting warmer with each passing minute. The sun sparkled on the Caribbean waters, and a gentle breeze made its way across the beach and carried with it the salty smell of the ocean. John Andrews sat back in his chair, watching, waiting, hoping for a sense of peace to settle over him.

It didn't.

By all accounts, he should have been content—a beachfront paradise, the woman he loved beside him, and a career's worth of success behind him. And yet, a question had been gnawing at him for months, refusing to let go.

What now?

Children shouted to their parents, "Hurry, look!" as they put the finishing touches on a sandcastle. They'd been at it all morning—it was massive. But the tide was rising, and with each wave, the ocean crept closer. They tried to hold it back with a small wall, but soon the water engulfed it. Moments later, the sandcastle's base gave way, collapsing in front of their eyes. Fortunately, their parents snapped a few photos before it was gone.

John, watching from a distance, felt a heaviness in his chest—a twinge of sadness. *Is that what happens to everything we build?* He'd spent his whole career at one company, and the thought that it too would one day vanish left him melancholy.

John had observed the whole scene with some fascination, reminiscing about times he'd built similar structures with his children. They were now grown and out of the house so this morning it was just he and his wife Abigail. They were both relaxing with a book, enjoying the rhythmic sounds of the ocean rolling in and out against the shore. Their annual getaway to St. John had always been a time to recharge, but this year, the stillness of the late morning felt less like rest and more like a void. John couldn't shake the question that had been hounding him for months, "What now?" As they lounged on the beach with toes dug into the warm sand, other vacationers began to settle in under the umbrellas, which the resort staff had meticulously planted across the beach about an hour earlier.

It had been 18 months since John left MediTech. Although he worked long hours, he was never what you might call a workaholic. For John, work was never about the paycheck. It was about influence—working with people to help them reach their potential, which was often more than they ever thought possible. His mind wandered back to Keri, a member of the corporate university he helped to overcome the fear of public speaking. It was a joy to see her excel, professionally and personally, from that point forward. He missed that feeling.

Now he and Abigail were enjoying the fruits of his successful career. Though 30 years sounds long, John had retired in his mid-50s. Suddenly, the thought struck, "Your career passed as quickly as that sandcastle. Nothing built on sand lasts forever."

He had his health and thought, God willing, he had a whole life ahead of him. He'd been the CEO at MediTech for 14 years so he and Abigail were financially secure, which meant he had options as to how he would spend his time and energy. While his current lot in life was a position most people aspired to, something was nagging at him. As he watched an elderly couple stroll down the beach, hand in hand, he thought, "They seem so content but I'm so restless. There has to be more to life than travel and relaxation from this point forward."

"What now?" That question had plagued him for months. He knew

Chapter 1 – What Now?

it wasn't a desire to go back to work. As important as work was, and the influence he'd had on people during his time at MediTech, he was at peace with his career in the rearview mirror. For a time, he thought his unease might just be a response to adjusting to a less hectic schedule, trying to find new, meaningful routines, or maybe a little boredom. But none of those seemed to explain why he was feeling discontent. As he stared out at the horizon he thought, "There has to be more to life going forward."

Abigail had been sharing things that were happening at church, including the chatter from some members who felt overwhelmed at always being asked for more money to fund new projects. She turned to John and realized he hadn't heard a word she was saying. He wasn't inconsiderate so she surmised something was on his mind. After 30 years of marriage, she knew him better than anyone, sometimes better than he knew himself, because the two had become one long ago.

"John," her use of his name caught his attention, "What's going through that mind of yours," she asked.

"Nothing much," he replied, unsure how to put his feelings into words.

She wasn't about to take that pat answer. She put her book down, placed her hand on his forearm, and turned to look at him. Once their eyes met, she said, "John, I know you almost as well as you know yourself so I can tell when you're wrestling with something. What's up?"

Trying to find the right words, he answered, "I love the life we have. We are blessed beyond what anyone deserves but I feel like there has to be more to life than vacations and relaxation going forward."

"More?" she said, indicating she had no idea where he might go with this. After a short pause she went on, "I know you're not into material things so what more could you want? You're not thinking of going back to work, are you?" She didn't want to see him go back to the grind of corporate life in any form or fashion. She'd shared him with so many people for so long over his career that she wanted to be his main focus, at least for the foreseeable future.

"No, I'm not looking to get back into the rat race," he assured her. "I loved my career but that's not what I'm looking for." After a short pause to collect his thoughts, he went on, "It's like … imagine an athlete who's spent decades training, finally wins gold, only to wake up the next morning thinking, 'What's next? Is this all there is?' That's me, Abigail. I loved what I did, but now that it's over, I can't shake this feeling that there's something more I'm supposed to do. Something bigger than myself."

She was secure in herself, her faith, and their relationship, so she knew John wasn't struggling with a mid-life crisis. He wasn't the kind of man who might want a red sports car and someone younger, but she wasn't sure what to make of that last comment.

Never one to mince words she simply asked, "What do you mean, 'Is this all there is?' You've led a good life, have positively influenced so many people, and helped countless others indirectly because of MediTech."

He responded, "I appreciate you saying that, and I believe it's true. I don't know what I mean just yet. It's hard to put into words, but I know the feeling."

Knowing this was not something that would be resolved in a short conversation, Abigail asked, "Have you talked to anyone about how you're feeling or prayed about it?"

John was a contemplative person, so it wasn't in his nature to do either until he felt like he'd looked at something from every angle. He thought, "How do you talk to someone about something when you can't define it for yourself?" Then he answered Abigail, "No, I've not done either, yet."

Abigail always seemed to know how to help John. Ever since they first met, she had been his confidant. Named after one of King David's wives, Abigail lived up to her namesake's wisdom—offering insight at just the right moment, often when John needed it most. She went on, "Can I give you a little advice?"

"Absolutely. You know I trust you," he replied.

"We're on vacation with no set plans, so take some time this week and begin praying about it. Your ability to influence people is a gift, John—the ability to guide others, to make a difference. Maybe this restlessness is God nudging you toward something bigger, something eternal. Pray about it. Let Him show you how to use the gifts He gave you."

John knew she was right. His thoughts returned to the sandcastle—and the fleeting nature of so much we build. He often leaned on his own understanding, perhaps more than he should. Most of the time that approach worked but this wasn't a business situation to be solved. It was deeper and more personal. "Thanks, I'll take some time each morning to do that. I appreciate you asking and listening because it's been on my mind for a while," he said, wondering why he'd not talked with her earlier.

A few days later, while reading, he came across Proverbs 3:5-6, "Trust in the Lord with all your heart and do not lean on your own understanding. In all your ways acknowledge Him, and He will make your paths straight."

As he contemplated the passage, he was reminded of one of the many stories he learned as a child at church. Abraham was called to go forth from his homeland but didn't know where he was going. He had to trust God's leading and in doing so became a model of faith for all time. John didn't see himself as the next Abraham, but he knew he could learn something from the man.

By the time their vacation was coming to a close, John was beginning to feel less anxious about the future. He remembered Jesus exhorting people to build their house on the rock, not sand. He no longer felt like he was on shifting sand. He was standing on the Rock. The path ahead was still uncertain, but for the first time in months, he felt at peace with the journey. He would wait—and trust.

> **Reflection:** John's question—"What now?"—is one we all face when life changes and former goals no longer satisfy. His reflection on the sandcastle reminds us that much of what we build in life, no matter how meaningful, won't last unless it's grounded in something eternal. Jesus called us to build on the Rock, not sand. When we surrender our plans and trust God's leading, He invites us into a purpose that transcends success—a life of lasting influence and eternal significance.

Chapter 2 – A Vision

*"Record the vision and inscribe it on tablets,
That the one who reads it may run.
For the vision is yet for the appointed time;
It hastens toward the goal and it will not fail."*

—Habakkuk 2:2–3

John had spent the past few weeks praying, just as Abigail had suggested. But if God had an answer, He wasn't making it obvious.

Then came Sunday morning.

John and Abigail lived in Clairemont, North Carolina, a quaint town about 30 minutes west of Charlotte. They'd moved there almost 20 years earlier when John accepted a role in the corporate university at Medi-Tech's home office. Established in 1838, Clairemont exuded Southern charm. With just over 17,000 residents, it was growing again because it was seen by many as a bedroom community for people working in Charlotte. Nonetheless, it retained its small town feel, especially with the shops and restaurants along Main Street, where business owners greeted you by name. It was the kind of town where most people knew each other and many residents had been there for several generations.

John and Abigail had been attending The Rock, a fairly large non-denominational church, for many years because faith had remained an important part of both of their lives since childhood. As they entered the church, the aroma of freshly brewed coffee greeted them. There was a murmur of voices as people socialized before the service

Chapter 2 – A Vision

began—familiar faces greeting each other, parents struggling with small children, and old friends embracing.

John and Abigail made their way to their usual seats near the middle of the sanctuary. The band played softly in the background, a melody of quiet worship to set the tone for what was to come.

The Rock focused on community outreach. The building was 15 years old and reminiscent of many non-denominational churches. Despite a sanctuary that could hold 1,200 people, the church had to start a second Sunday morning service a few years ago. Not only did it accommodate growth, but it also gave people flexibility, which was especially appreciated by parents with small children. The main stage was set up to accommodate a choir or band, depending on the theme of the service. There were big screens on both sides of the stage to allow people to follow the sermon outline or see the words to the worship songs.

The lobby's coffee shop and bookstore created a welcoming space for mingling, while classrooms hosted Bible studies and community groups throughout the week.

In his early 50s, Senior Pastor Dennis Reacher had spent years in the Peace Corps before answering the call to ministry. What began as a small Bible study in his home had grown into The Rock, a thriving church built on faith in action. He and his wife, Amanda, were raising two boys, ages 10 and 13.

Dennis was generally a soft spoken man but there was definitely a difference in his demeanor when he preached. He wasn't fire-and-brimstone, and nor did he resemble a television preacher. However, you would feel his passion and excitement the further he got into his sermon.

He believed true faith would manifest itself in good works. He often quoted James 2:18 from the pulpit, "You have faith, and I have works; show me your faith without the works, and I will show you my faith by my works." It wasn't a legalistic approach, but rather a way of putting the teachings of Jesus into practice to impact people positively. To that end, some church activities included family movie nights, car washes once a month, and raising money for school supplies for families in financial need. None of the activities were limited to church members. In fact, there were more non-members who were beneficiaries of the free activities, which is exactly what Dennis was hoping for.

With the kids grown and out of the house, Abigail used much of her free time to get actively involved in many of the outreach events. John, on the other hand, limited his participation to Sunday mornings, which was understandable because he had little free time while he was running MediTech. What he lacked in participation he made up for by generously contributing financially to the church and various ministries. Now that he was retired, he had an opportunity to give and volunteer.

On this particular Sunday morning, Dennis laid out a vision for a community center. "The goal is simple but profound," Dennis said. "Imagine a place where kids can go after school—kids who might otherwise be on the streets or home alone. A place where they're mentored, learn life skills, and build meaningful relationships. Parents will know their children are safe. Teens from broken homes will have role models. And the entire community will benefit from a generation that grows up with hope."

Dennis painted a stirring picture, "Imagine a boy named Tommy walking into the community center after school—his mom works two jobs to make ends meet, and he has nowhere to go once the school day is over. He doesn't say much at first, just sits in the corner, watching the other kids. Then a volunteer strikes up a conversation. Before you know it, Tommy is showing up every day. He gets help with his homework or maybe he plays basketball with friends. Both are better alternatives to running the streets. And one day, he realizes something—he's part of a family."

A stirring rose within John—one he hadn't felt since those early, uncertain days as CEO at MediTech. He could almost see the center—a bustling building filled with kids laughing, volunteers teaching, and families connecting. For a moment, his mind raced with ideas: fundraising strategies, mentorship programs, outreach events. But then a voice in the back of his head whispered—"What do you know about running a ministry?"

Chapter 2 – A Vision

Fundraising, strategy, leadership—those, he understood. But ministry? That was foreign territory.

When he ran MediTech, he had sales reports, balance sheets, and other metrics to consult. Success was definable and measurable. His mind went back to when Bob McMillen was let go for embezzlement and he took over as interim CEO. He was in uncharted waters and had no blueprint for success. But by the end of the first quarter, despite the public nature of Bob's scandal, John guided MediTech to quarterly records in both sales and profit. But a community center? How do you quantify changed lives? What if all their effort led to nothing? Failing at business was one thing—but failing people? That was different.

So, he had doubts on one hand but felt like he shared Dennis's vision on the other hand. The more he focused on the vision, the more he felt as if it already existed in his mind.

Then Abigail's elbow nudged him, breaking in on his thoughts.

"This might be what you're looking for," she whispered. "You know how to take a vision and make it come to life."

As they were getting ready to head home, Dennis waived to John and Abigail as he made his way toward them. When he arrived, he shook John's hand and hugged Abigail. She said, "Dennis, I have to be honest, if the community center project comes about, it will be a challenge primarily from within. People are feeling financially stressed. We just finished paying off the sanctuary remodel and many are hoping for a little breathing room."

Dennis smiled. "If we had all the answers, where would faith fit in?" He turned to John. "How's retired life treating you? It's been over a year, right?"

John nodded. "A year and a half, actually. Being out of the rat race has been good. I never realized how much pressure there was until I stepped away. It's a little like watching a scary movie. You don't realize how tense you are until the movie is over, you're leaving the theater, and you finally exhale."

"I get it," Dennis said. "Running a big church isn't like running a major company but there's always something weighing on me." He went on, "John, I have to tell you, as I prayed about this community center, your name kept coming to mind. I can't think of anyone better suited to take this vision and turn it into reality. You have a gift. You've spent decades leading people, solving problems, and inspiring others to do more than they thought they could. What if everything you've done—every challenge, every victory—was preparation for this?"

John was clearly flattered. After a short pause, Dennis made a simple ask, "All I'd like you to do is pray about it, John. Will you do that for me?"

The ask didn't catch John off guard because truth be told, the thought of working in some capacity with the community center entered his mind as Dennis shared his vision with the congregation. While John thought this might be the answer to the question he'd been pondering and praying about during vacation, he still had doubts. Again, a voice inside his head said, "What do you know about ministry?" Church work seemed very different than the kind of work he was used to as a businessman, at least in his mind.

As the conversation continued, one of the "Clyde-isms" he'd learned at the beginning of his career popped into his mind, "There's always three things." Between the thought in the pew, Abigail's elbow, and Dennis's ask—three promptings.

"I get it," John said, a faint smile breaking through. "Three promptings. I'll pray about it, Dennis. I promise."

Dennis and Abigail exchanged smiles, knowing what was happening. They could see God at work in John's life, even if he didn't realize it just yet.

They walked to the car and Abigail continued to speak excitedly about the project. "John, this might be what you're looking for—a chance to lead and influence people's lives in a whole new way."

As the excitement was wearing off and "rational" thoughts hit John, he shook his head. "Running a business wasn't easy but I had nearly two decades of work experience behind me before I became CEO. I don't know anything about leading a church project."

"How much did you really know about running a company? You've been attending church most of your life so there's more experience in there," she pointed to his head, "to help you navigate this than you might realize."

John smiled at that because she was always his biggest fan.

Abigail went on, "Do you remember the car wash last month, where the woman whose husband just left her stopped by? By the end of the wash, she was in tears, hugging some of the volunteers. It wasn't her car that needed cleaned, it was her heart because of the bitterness she was holding on to."

By now they were pulling out of the parking lot. John turned to Abigail and said, "I told Dennis I'd pray about it—and I will."

Abigail squeezed his hand, a knowing smile on her lips. "If this is God's vision, He'll make it clear—He always does."

> **Reflection:** Like John, we all face moments when we sense a calling beyond our comfort zone. What if the skills and experiences you've gained were never just about career success—but about preparing you to influence lives in a way that echoes into eternity? Are you open to seeing your "next chapter" through God's eyes?

Chapter 3 – Laying Out His Fleece

"Behold, I will put a fleece of wool on the threshing floor. If there is dew on the fleece only, and it is dry on all the ground, then I will know that You will deliver Israel through me, as You have spoken."

—Judges 6:37

John knew that desire and encouragement—even when well-intentioned—didn't necessarily equal God's will. The community center project would be big, maybe even bigger than Dennis realized—and that thought both excited and terrified John. Unlike many activities The Rock did for outreach, this project wouldn't be limited to the church. It would necessitate building relationships outside the church, throughout the community. Based on his extensive career running MediTech, John knew the biggest hurdles might be the city council and zoning board.

In his experience, most council members first asked, "What's in it for me?"—and only then, "What's in it for the community?" To John's knowledge, no one in either group was a member of The Rock. On top of that, he'd heard rumblings that some were openly against faith-based projects because they were seen as exclusionary or just a cover for proselytizing in the community.

True to his word, John began to pray about it. Days went by, then weeks but John didn't feel like he was getting any direction. He began to get discouraged. One night, as he lay in bed he wondered, "Does God really answer specific prayers—or only for people more spiritual than me?"

Chapter 3 – Laying Out His Fleece

One morning, John sat on the edge of the bed. The room was dark and quiet, and Abigail was still in a deep sleep. His whispered prayer felt small compared to the spacious bedroom. "God, I need a sign. Something clear. I don't want to move unless it's from You."

But every morning, he woke up with the same uncertainty. He wanted to believe God was listening, but with each passing day, he wondered if his prayers were just words floating into the void. He'd heard of answered prayers from friends, but he'd also heard of just as many that were not answered. He began to wonder if answered prayer was as random as the flip of a coin.

Since leaving MediTech, he'd joined a men's group that focused on reading through the entire Bible in a year. The small group of eight men met every Tuesday evening from 6 till 8. After a simple meal, the rest of the time was focused on discussing that week's chapters and sharing what was going on in their lives. It was one of John's favorite times of the week. Not only did he enjoy the men, but also reading through the Bible brought back happy memories of childhood when he and his brother Billy and sister Carey went to church with their parents. The yearly reading plan also prompted him to remember many stories he'd first learned at youth groups and Bible camps. One story that came to mind this particular day had to do with Gideon.

Gideon was a nobody from the smallest of the 12 tribes of Israel. One day, he felt the call of God to lead his people out from under the oppression of the Midianites. Because of his lowly stature and the power of the Midianites, Gideon understandably had doubts. He turned to God for a sign. He placed a wool fleece on the ground and asked God to make the fleece wet with dew but to keep the ground dry. That oddity would surely be a sign. God did so but still doubting, Gideon asked God the next day to make the fleece dry and the ground full of dew. In other words, reverse the order God. Again, God answered, and this time Gideon knew the Lord was with him. With only 300 men, Gideon defeated an army of 135,000!

John prayed that God would give him a clear sign, just as he'd done with Gideon. The difference was that John didn't specify what God needed to do. He trusted God would make it clear in time. He shared this with Abigail and asked that she would include it in her prayers, which she happily agreed to do.

***

Later that week, Abigail asked if John would run to the grocery store for her. Truthfully, John didn't want to because no matter how hard he tried, he always seemed to come home with something that was wrong. The canned goods were too big or small, it wasn't the brand Abigail used when cooking, or sometimes he just missed something on the list. However, he set aside his reservation and agreed to help out.

As John pulled into the parking lot, he sighed, not wanting to be there. He parked, grabbed the list, and slowly made his way toward the entrance. That's when he noticed an older man standing near the doors, holding a small stack of books. The man's skin was weathered; his face looked a little like leather because of the sun-worn lines beneath the shadow of a faded Boston Red Sox ballcap. His jacket, once blue, had faded to a muted gray, the pockets frayed from years of use. It was apparent from his physical appearance and his clothing; he spent a good bit of time outside in the elements. Most people walked by trying to avoid eye contact, muttering polite, "No thank yous." John decided he'd follow the lead of the other patrons.

As John got closer, he could see the man was trying to give away Bibles. John was fully prepared to politely decline the offer, but something the man said grabbed his attention.

The older man said with humility in his voice, "Hey mister, would you like a *Gideon* Bible?"

It was as if God Himself had spoken, stopping John in his tracks. *Of all the names ... of all the moments!* It momentarily took his breath away, and he felt a strange sensation course his body. What were the odds that he'd been praying about Gideon's fleece and now this? He turned and asked the man in stunned disbelief, "What did you say?"

The man wasn't sure how to read John based on his tone, so he sheepishly replied, "I … I wasn't trying to offend you. I just asked if you would like a Gideon Bible? They're free."

John reached out his hand and graciously accepted the gift, saying, "I would really appreciate that, sir." As John held the Bible in his hands, scanning the black cover and gold letters, he thought of Gideon's fleece, damp with dew while the ground around it was dry. God had spoken then, and He was speaking now. John's voice trembled just a bit, "You have no idea—but you just answered a prayer."

The old man's eyes widened, a hint of moisture gathering at the corners. "I had a feeling someone needed one," he whispered. "But I never imagined it'd be something this big."

"How many have you given away today," John inquired.

"None until now. You're my only one," he answered then went on, "Been out here several hours and was about to pack up but I felt a strong sense that someone really needed one of these Bibles, so I stuck around."

"I'm glad you did!" John exclaimed. "How much do these cost you?"

The old man replied, "They're only $5 each, but like I said earlier, I give 'em away for free."

"What's your name?" John asked with a sincerity in his voice that made the old man feel comfortable.

"My family calls me Josh, but I prefer Joshua," he said with a hint of pride, knowing he was named after the biblical character who led the Israelites into the promised land.

"Joshua, nice to meet you, I'm John." They shook hands. "I'll tell you what," John said as he opened his wallet, "I want to give you $50 so you can add to your supply. I have a feeling you might need them for other folks," he said in anticipation of God using Joshua in other people's lives.

Joshua tried to resist but John insisted and finally persuaded him to take the $50 bill. He didn't realize until John disappeared into the store that he'd actually slipped two 50s in his hand, knowing Joshua might need a new jacket in the not too distant future. He stood there and began to cry, knowing God had used him to answer a random stranger's prayer and the generosity of that same stranger. Both men were better off for having met one another.

True to form, John messed up the grocery list a little, but Abigail couldn't have cared less. Her eyes filled with tears as John shared details about his encounter with Joshua. "I've heard stories like this," she said. "When people ask God for a sign, and He shows up in ways they never expected."

"It wasn't just a sign," John said. "It was personal—like God had been listening all along. I have no doubt Joshua felt the same."

Abigail reached for her Bible, which was full of handwritten notes and colored highlights. She turned the pages until she landed on a verse. "Listen to this, John," she said excitedly. "Isaiah 30:21—'Your ears will hear a word behind you, "This is the way, walk in it," whenever you turn to the right or to the left.' I think this is your path, John."

The whole experience reminded John of another time God intervened in his life, even if he didn't see it as clearly as the encounter with Joshua. Early in his tenure as CEO, MediTech was on the brink of a major acquisition, but something hadn't felt right to John. He couldn't put his finger on it, but he felt something in the pit of his stomach. Against the advice of his board, he had paused negotiations, taking time to pray and seek wisdom. Days later, before making a final decision, his accounting team uncovered a hidden financial risk that could have sunk the company had the deal gone through. It was a defining moment, the first time John learned to trust that still, small voice over the loud logic of the boardroom and senior advisors. He hadn't realized it then, but God had been training him for something more—for a moment like this.

John and Abigail knew their prayers had been answered so John decided to call Dennis first thing in the morning to accept the assignment. Later that night, as John sat by his bedroom window, the small Gideon Bible rested on his nightstand. He opened it, not sure where to start, and landed on Proverbs 16:9, "The mind of man plans his way, but the Lord directs his steps."

He closed his eyes. "God, I'm listening. Lead me." And for the first time in months, John felt not just hope—but calling.

It did not escape his notice that he'd been *Influenced from Above*.

Reflection: John's request for a sign reminds us that seeking God's will often comes with uncertainty—and yet, God graciously meets us where we are. Like Gideon, John felt unqualified and unsure, but through a seemingly random encounter, God spoke with clarity. In our own lives, answers may not come in thunder or lightning but through unexpected moments—a word, a person, a circumstance—that remind us God sees, hears, and guides. When we're willing to slow down and listen, we find that His direction is both personal and purposeful.

Chapter 4 – Responding to the Call

*"Then I heard the voice of the Lord, saying,
'Whom shall I send, and who will go for Us?'
Then I said, 'Here am I. Send me!'"*

—Isaiah 6:8

Abigail was just as thrilled as John about his encounter the day before. She'd had moments when God spoke clearly to her—through Scripture, a song, or an unexpected word from a friend—and she knew how powerful those moments could be. John had taught her so much about influence, and now, in matters of faith, she felt blessed to reciprocate.

As they milled around the kitchen the next morning in anticipation of their days, she told John, "You know, I remember a time I was really struggling, feeling alone. I'd been praying for weeks, asking God if He saw me, if He cared. Then, one afternoon driving to pick up the kids at school, a song came on—something about God leaving the 99 to find the one. I sat there in the car, crying. I knew He was speaking to me."

John stood there, listening in amazement. He could relate because his understanding that God speaks to us was moving from his head to his heart.

"And there was another time," Abigail continued, "when I was thinking about joining the outreach team at church. I felt completely unqualified, but then a friend, without even knowing that I was wrestling with self-doubt, told me, 'You have a gift for making people feel seen

Chapter 4 – Responding to the Call

and valued.' She probably had no clue, but it was like God was speaking directly through her. I knew then that I needed to step out in faith."

"Those are incredible stories," John said, surprised that she'd never shared them earlier. "Why didn't you share those stories before?" he asked.

"Honestly, I wasn't sure you could relate," she told him. She couldn't resist saying next, "But now that you can, maybe you should go to the grocery store for me every week."

As excited as John was about his encounter, he let her know that might not happen as often as she'd like. She looked at him with a frown then they both laughed.

Shortly after getting his coffee, John made his way to his office to ready himself for the call. He sat down in his big, leather chair and thought for a moment. Although he felt he'd received the sign he needed, there were still nagging thoughts. "This isn't business, this is church," and "Are you really up for this?" were most persistent. Finally, he pushed aside the doubts and dialed the number.

"Dennis, I think God gave me my sign," John said, his voice a mixture of nerves and excitement.

"I'm all ears," Dennis replied, anticipating a God encounter story. He preached that God is a personal Being who cares so much for each of us that He has the very hairs on our head numbered. He loved it when people in his flock experienced God in ways that made Him real for each of them individually.

John excitedly told him about his specific prayer and the encounter with Joshua, the old man handing out the Gideon Bibles at the grocery store. "It wasn't exactly a burning bush," he said, "but it was nearly the same for me." Although John couldn't see Dennis, because he'd gotten to know him a little better, he could sense a smile on the other end of the phone and heard him chuckle more than once.

"John, I experienced something similar before starting The Rock," Dennis said. "I was volunteering in the Peace Corps in Costa Rica. One day, out of the blue, a local pastor said in broken English, 'Dennis, have heart for people. God will use you in way you cannot imagine.' I was flattered but I didn't think much of it. However, looking back, I realized that was the moment God planted the seed for this church."

John got goosebumps. If Dennis had not obeyed his calling, John and Abigail's lives, along with so many others at The Rock, would be very different.

Dennis went on, "John, God speaks to us all the time. However, because it's seldom a burning bush encounter like Moses had, most people miss it or pass it off as coincidence. If you keep your heart open, listening with your eyes and ears, you'll be amazed as He keeps speaking to you."

Dennis paused, then continued, "Let me put it this way. Imagine being at a crowded party—music blaring, voices everywhere—then, amid the noise, you hear your name. No one else notices, but you do. That's how God speaks. It's personal, and unmistakable. I don't think there's anything more exciting in life than to know the creator of heaven and earth cares enough to speak to us individually. And believe me, you'll need His guidance with this project."

John understood what Dennis meant about listening with his eyes and ears. He'd learned a long time ago that people missed influence opportunities that were readily apparent to John and others who were skilled influencers. That was because most people had little understanding of the language of persuasion and what it takes to influence people ethically.

John had no idea that Dennis foreshadowed what was to come with his last sentence. He was on a spiritual high and let Dennis know that he'd never experienced anything like that before. He told Dennis that he'd attended church since childhood and, while he believed in God and prayer, sensing God spoke directly to him was new. He felt like things he understood intellectually suddenly covered the longest distance anyone on a journey of transformation travels, from his head to his heart. It was also intimidating. "Dennis, to be honest, it's a little scary when I think about it."

"That's natural, John. I think it's one reason the psalmist wrote, 'The fear of the Lord is the beginning of wisdom,'" Dennis assured him in an encouraging tone.

Chapter 4 – Responding to the Call

"So, what now?" John asked.

"The first step," Dennis said, "will be to meet with me and Dave Sargent to begin strategizing. Dave will be the church liaison. I'll set that up. After that, you and Dave will start meeting with people—learn their needs, hear their stories. This project isn't just about a building; it's about building relationships."

As soon as they hung up, John pulled his well-worn copy of Robert Cialdini's *Influence: The Psychology of Persuasion* from his bookshelf; its pages were dog eared, marked with notes and highlights. He flipped to the chapter on reciprocity, a principle he'd used effectively throughout his business career.

"Do unto others as you would have them do unto you," he thought, reminding him of Christ's words in Luke 6:31. Next, he opened his Bible, and placed the two books side by side. For the first time, the connection was clear—one was a principle of persuasion, the other, a spiritual principle. Different sources, same truth. Could it be that the principles of influence were not just psychological tools but also spiritual truths? The thought excited him because he loved studying both topics.

Later that evening, over dinner John and Abigail continued their conversation about God's influence in their lives. Then Abigail posed a question no one had ever asked John before. "John, I've seen you use influence as a tool to ethically impact people for as long as I've known you. But I've always wondered—where does God fit into the principles of influence you use?"

That wasn't something John had ever given thought to prior to opening the two books side by side a few minutes earlier. He knew the principles of influence he'd learned about as a freshman in college—then seen as so effective in his career and personal life—could be tools for good. They certainly were for him. However, they could also be used by unscrupulous individuals to manipulate people just to get what they wanted. John briefly thought about Rich Bennett, a salesman he had to shadow early in his career while in training. Rich, who went by the nickname "Flick," would say or do anything, including telling outright lies, to land a sales deal. He was the kind of salesman people dreaded—slick, smooth-talking, untrustworthy. As clients caught on, he moved on, always landing new sales roles before his reputation caught up to him again.

John thought, "Unfortunately, people often used religion in the same way—to get what they wanted and to control people." The Pharisees were the ultimate example of this, using the Law to control people rather than point them to God. This is why, when speaking of the Pharisees, Jesus warned his followers, "Therefore all that they tell you, do and observe, but do not do according to their deeds; for they say things and do not do them" (Matthew 23:3). Their lack of consistency in word and deed is what made them hypocrites. Jesus, however, did all that He encourages us to do, even sacrificing His own life to demonstrate the highest form of love.

This brought to mind a quote from Shakespeare that John had often referred to, "There's nothing good or bad, but thinking makes it so." The principles of influence were neither good nor bad; they simply described how people typically thought and behaved. How people used them revealed their characters, but it's the Lord who weighs our motives (Proverbs 16:2). The famous Greek philosopher Aristotle also knew this well and advised listeners thousands of years ago, "Character may almost be called the most effective means of persuasion."

John leaned back in his chair, a smile slowly spreading across his face. For so long, he'd thought of influence as a tool for sales and leadership, a way to guide decisions and shape outcomes. But now, he was starting to see it as something sacred—a means to serve, to love, to draw people toward God.

"This is bigger than a building," he whispered. "It's about building the Kingdom—one relationship at a time."

It was at this point that John decided to devote his morning quiet time to explore the relationship between the principles of influence and faith before diving into the community center project. He knew some people mistakenly thought influence was just a nice word for manipulation. While he'd never held that view, he believed there might be something even deeper to ethical influence than he realized. Spiritual influence might be the key he was looking for, the connection between faith and influence.

Suddenly everything was coming together. He felt inspired because he knew in the deepest part of his being that he had purpose again.

> **Reflection:** When God calls us, He rarely reveals the whole path—only the next step. It's called walking by faith. Like John, we often hesitate, wondering if we're qualified or equipped. But calling isn't about our ability; it's about God's purpose and our willingness to be used by Him. Influence, rightly used, becomes a sacred trust—a way to love, serve, and point others to God. True purpose comes when we see that our gifts are not just for professional success or personal happiness, but for Kingdom impact.

Chapter 5 – Where is God?

"I do all things for the sake of the gospel."

—1 Corinthians 19:23

John had always loved his home office, especially in the early mornings. During his career, it served as a quiet refuge—a place where ideas took shape and strategies were born. Many of MediTech's greatest innovations began under the soft glow of his desk lamp, the only light in an otherwise dark room lined with mahogany bookshelves. John would only turn on his desk light once he was seated with his coffee. He liked the sense of isolation the single light created because it helped him to avoid distractions, allowing him to focus.

With his career behind him, the office was beginning to feel more like a sanctuary because he used it for morning quiet time as he read and prayed. Now it was expanding with his studies about faith and influence.

When it came to studying, that was never a problem for John. He had enjoyed learning, even back in high school, as long as the topic was interesting and relevant. The influence–faith connection met both criteria, so he looked forward to digging in and learning. It wasn't so much about memorizing facts as it was making connections between disparate ideas. Those connections seemed to open new possibilities in his mind.

He sipped his coffee and quietly prayed, "God, let me hear Your voice today. Help me see the connections You want me to make."

As he sat there a thought struck him, "Character and intent are inseparable—they're the source of our actions," he mused.

Chapter 5 – Where is God?

Reaching for his Bible, he opened it and turned to Proverbs 16:2. The passage shares a profound truth on the intentions of the heart, "All the ways of a man are clean in his own sight, but the Lord weighs the motives." Jesus said as much when He told the Pharisees they needed to clean the inside of the cup, their hearts, then the outside of the cup, their actions, would be clean. He tapped his pen as he pondered these connections. He'd seen many times during his career where people felt passionately about making a sale or convincing people to take on a new strategic initiative, believing their motives were right, only to find out later they were driven more by self-interest. Situations like those usually hurt clients and the company because self-interest took priority over what was best for others.

His mind drifted back to a leadership training session he'd led when he ran MediTech's corporate university. He'd been teaching the principle of liking, encouraging managers to find genuine connections with their teams. One participant raised a hand and asked, "So, we get people to like us, so they'll do what we want?" The question had a manipulative undertone.

"No," John had replied. "We build real relationships so we can serve people better. Influence isn't a shortcut to success—it's a path to trust and connection."

Now, sitting in his study, John realized that this same approach could be the key to the community center project. If he approached influence with a servant's heart, it could become a tool for ministry, not just a strategy for success.

A bit of a pack rat, he'd kept his notes on the principles of influence from his college days because they were such an important part of his life, success, and happiness. As he looked at them, fond memories of college washed over him. He'd been somewhat shy in high school but had decided to step out of his shell in college. No one knew him there, and he realized he could become whomever he wanted to be with a fresh start. Call it good fortune, or perhaps divine intervention, the principles were the single biggest factor that shaped who he became. "I wonder if God's hand was in that," he thought.

A few moments passed; then, his focus turned to the old notepad in his hands as he reclined in his leather chair. Below was what he wrote on the yellow legal pad during that Psych 101 class he took as a freshman nearly four decades earlier.

- *Liking* – If people like you, they'll say yes to you.
- *Unity* – People you share a deep connection with are more likely to say yes to you.
- *Reciprocity* – Be a giver if you ever hope to get.
- *Social Proof* – Talk about what other people are doing.
- *Authority* – If an expert says it, people are more likely to believe it.
- *Consistency* – People feel good about themselves when they keep their word.
- *Scarcity* – People respond to the fear of missing out.
- *Contrast* – Make good comparisons so people notice differences.

Early in his career, he viewed the principles primarily as an avenue to success. It wasn't that they were simply a means to an end, but coming out of college and starting a career, success was his main focus. Later he began to connect the dots between different principles—when to use certain ones, how they informed each other, how they could amplify one another when used together—he felt like he was putting a puzzle together. It wasn't until near the end of his career that he finally saw the puzzle picture—influence was all about people. Eventually it came to him in a eureka moment—PEOPLE was an acronym that stood for Powerful Everyday Opportunities to Persuade that are Lasting and Ethical.

For a moment, he questioned whether bringing a business concept like influence into ministry was appropriate. Could it be misunderstood? Could it crowd out faith? But then he realized—it wasn't about influence or faith versus each other; it was about intent. Influence, guided by love and truth, could serve others—and serve God.

He pondered the principle of liking. Used properly, liking wasn't about getting people to like you so you could simply get what you

Chapter 5 – Where is God?

wanted. It was about coming to genuinely like others, so you'd want to help them. If he could tie spiritual realities to his understanding of influence in the way that he'd done with liking early in his career, his approach would go much deeper because it would be about service to others and to God. Suddenly he realized that this could have eternal consequences.

He shared the focus of his study with Dennis because of his respect for his pastor. Dennis encouraged him to look into Dallas Willard's work. Willard was a Christian philosopher who'd spent most of his career at the University of Southern California. As Dennis talked about Willard, what was of particular interest to John was Willard's view on the human heart, mind, body, and soul.

John preferred physical books but decided to download a copy of *Renovation of the Heart* that afternoon because he was so excited to dive into it after hearing Dennis talk so enthusiastically about the book. Willard's words were gentle but piercing at times. They carried a spiritual weight that John had not encountered before. He found himself reading some sections multiple times because there was such depth to Willard's writing. It was as if every paragraph contained nuggets of spiritual gold. Sitting at his desk, surrounded by several books and lots of paper, all he could focus on was the idea that the heart is the executive center of a person.

For Willard, the heart—sometimes referred to as the spirit or will—is the place of our deepest beliefs and desires, from which everything originates. He recognized that the mind drives behavior through conscious and unconscious decisions. The body, the primary place of feelings, carries out the intentions of the heart and mind. It's how we present ourselves to the world. But the body also has "a mind of its own," so to speak, because of its habitual conditioning throughout life. Willard's view of the soul was that it integrated the heart, mind, and body into a unified whole for each person.

As John pondered this, he began to see high-level connections between the principles and Willard's view of the human. As he sat at his desk in his study, which was lined with books, pictures, and mementos from friends and former colleagues, he reached for a pen and began writing. He enjoyed scribbling ideas on paper before sitting at his computer to refine his thoughts.

Relationships are formed at the heart level. The principles of liking and reciprocity are relationship builders, so they naturally fit with Willard's concept of the heart. The more we like people, the more they tend to like us in return and that kickstarts friendships. When we engage reciprocity by helping people in authentic ways, they appreciate it and want to return the favor. With a sincere desire to help or give, both parties benefit so it tends to enhance relationships.

Social proof and authority play to the mind. Intellectually, we're prone to follow people we view as experts. Two people can say the same thing but it's the expert who's typically believed. Humans also learned long ago that following the lead of similar others usually works out well because it enhances our survival as a species.

The body is heavily impacted by scarcity and consistency. Both of these principles are primarily driven by internal feelings. When it comes to scarcity, research from Daniel Kahneman and Amos Tversky statistically proved that people hate the feeling of loss so much that they're twice as likely to act when they think they'll lose something as when they can gain the same opportunity. Consistency is a natural internal motivation to follow through on commitments. We feel better about ourselves when we keep our word. It's strengthened further by the positive feelings that come with looking good in the eyes of others when we live up to our promises.

Unity, the seventh principle, seemed to be a natural fit for the soul in John's eyes. Unity is about sharing deep bonds, or having a shared identity, with others. It's the closest to love of any of the principles. Love is about doing what's best for others, even when it entails personal sacrifice. When we have unity with others, helping them is almost like helping ourselves.

John intuitively understood the importance of these connections. He knew from his long career that you don't treat everyone the same, and sometimes you say the same thing, but very differently, to people because of their roles or personality types. The same thoughtful approach would be necessary when dealing with people inside the church and outside that tightknit community. He would need to meet people where they were—inside the church and beyond. To serve them well, he'd have to be, in Paul's words, "all things to all people," for the sake of the community center—and for something far greater.

John exhaled, feeling the weight of his thoughts and the promise of purpose. The yellow notepad lay on his desk, a mixture of old notes and fresh insights.

"Thinking is hard work," a quote he recalled from Henry Ford. But beneath his mental fatigue was a sense of excitement. Now he understood Jesus's words, "Every scribe who becomes a disciple of the kingdom brings out of his treasure things new and old" (Matthew 15:32). God was weaving something new from the threads of his past. Tomorrow, the pattern would become clearer.

> **Reflection:** Like David, as a young man playing with a slingshot while tending the sheep, God often uses the skills and experiences we've accumulated in life—not to elevate ourselves, but for His glory. Much like John, we may wonder if our "secular" expertise fits into God's work. But when our motives are grounded in love and service, influence becomes a sacred tool. As we bring both old wisdom and new insight into His hands, we discover that God is not only present—He is the One weaving it all together for eternal purposes.

Chapter 6 – Biblical Influence

> *"All Scripture is inspired by God and profitable for teaching, for reproof, for correction, for training in righteousness; so that the man of God may be adequate, equipped for every good work."*
>
> —*2 Timothy 3:16–17*

John, always a morning person, woke up earlier than usual, eager to return to his study. The house was still and quiet, save for a few birds chirping and the occasional dog barking in the distance. Abigail remained asleep upstairs. John loved this early solitude—it was when his mind felt fresh, full of possibility. He was more excited than usual on this particular day.

He made his way downstairs to the spacious kitchen. He hit the grinder, gazing out into the early morning darkness as the rich aroma of coffee filled the kitchen. After a few minutes he reached for his favorite mug, poured the coffee then salted it with a little sugar and cream. After a sip to ensure it was to his liking, he headed into his office.

His notebook and pen were still sitting on his desk, just as he'd left them the day before. "Lord, thank You for yesterday's insights. I'm listening—show me more today," he prayed.

On a fresh piece of paper, he listed each of the principles again then opened his Bible to start looking for more connections to spiritual truths.

Liking. John had a habit of looking to Proverbs for wisdom. As he flipped the pages, Proverbs 17:17 seemed to jump off the page, "A friend loves at all times, and a brother is born for adversity." John was well aware that if people liked him, it was easier for them to say yes. That was the essence of friendship, as described in Proverbs.

Jesus modeled true friendship because He loved consistently and regardless of circumstance. And His love wasn't limited to those who were like Him in word or deed, or those He only felt positively towards.

John recalled the interaction Jesus had with Zacchaeus, the little tax collector who climbed a tree just to get a glimpse of Him. Jesus didn't preach to him from a distance. Instead, He asked to enter his home so He could share a meal and forge a connection. This was big because the Jews looked at tax collectors as collaborators with the Romans, their hated occupiers. It was through this genuine relationship that Zacchaeus's life changed, showing that influence often begins with a sincere desire to get to know someone.

This principle was a foundation for John, and he knew it would be more important than ever to win people over for the community center.

Reciprocity. John always thought of his former neighbor, Bud, when he contemplated reciprocity. Bud embodied, "Treat others the same way you want them to treat you," (Luke 6:31) and "It is more blessed to give than to receive" (Acts 20:35).

John immediately saw the connection back to liking. The more you come to like someone, the easier it is to give, and the more authentic your giving will be because you naturally want to help those you consider friends. Jesus embodied this when He washed His disciples' feet. It wasn't just an act of service; it was a model of how leaders should serve others first. His act of humility created a reciprocal sense of service among His disciples that would eventually expand to everyone they encountered.

John recalled all the times he would invite employees over for dinner at his home, especially those who traveled in from out of town. It was one thing to go to a nice restaurant, but it was much more intimate for executives to invite people to their homes.

"How can I embody this principle in a way that points people to Christ?" John jotted down.

Authority. When it comes to authority, we feel more confident following the lead of experts because they typically know more than we do. Following legitimate authorities usually saves us time, energy, and money.

Jesus was the ultimate example of authority. He had no money, power, or position in the worldly sense, but He had authority. That was so because of who He was, how He lived, and what He taught. That's why Luke 4:32 tells us, "They were amazed at His teaching, for His message was delivered with authority." Jesus's authority came because He always spoke the truth.

He also demonstrated authority when He calmed the storm (Mark 4:39) and healed the sick. His deeds validated all that He taught. This blend of truth and action built His influence.

And consider this—Jesus, the one who was given authority over all things, lived under the authority of His Father. A couple of notable places we see this come in Matthew 3:17, His baptism, and Matthew 17:5, His Transfiguration.

But there was a flip side to this. John knew that people don't always like hearing the truth because it often goes against what they want, which can lead to a sense of conviction. John wrote, "No one who truly loves you will lie to you."

Social Proof. John considered the power of social proof—the tendency of people to follow the lead of others. He recalled his mom warning him against caving to peer pressure. Just because everyone was doing something didn't always mean it was the right thing to do. He'd learned that lesson the hard way when he was 12 years old. He got in trouble for participating with friends who decided to egg a neighbor's house. He knew it was wrong but joined his buddies, nonetheless. Only later did he realize that it was just because he wanted to fit in.

However, social proof can be used to encourage good behavior and that's why the writer of Hebrews encourages us, "Therefore, since we have so great a cloud of witnesses surrounding us, let us also lay aside every encumbrance" (Hebrews 12:1). Those witnesses were proof of God's faithfulness for all time.

In Acts 2, the early Christians devoted themselves to the apostles' teaching, fellowship, and sharing meals. They also devoted themselves to one another, as many sold their possessions and shared with anyone who had need. They didn't do this for show, but their actions were still observed. People took note of how they loved one another, and that drew them to the faith.

This reminded John of the team he built when he ran MediTech's corporate university. They got along so well and helped each other in ways that caught the attention of other employees. It was a big reason so many inquired about working for John.

Consistency. "Let your yes be yes, and your no, no," (Matthew 5:37) was the essence of consistency. It was more than following through to get what you wanted or to look good. People feel better about themselves, and look good to others, when they follow through on their word. They are viewed as people of integrity and good character; the kind of individuals people naturally are inclined to follow.

The parable of the two sons in Matthew 21:28–31 illustrates the power of consistency. The son who followed through on his father's request was the one who honored him, showing that actions truly matter more than words.

John recognized it wasn't only about him using the principle when communicating with others; he too needed to be consistent to build trust quickly. His note to himself was, "Be dependable because people follow those they trust."

Scarcity. This principle often felt like a negative force—fear of missing out, a gnawing sense of loss. But John saw how Jesus used urgency for good, reminding His disciples of the fleeting opportunity to do God's work in John 9:4, "We must work the works of Him who sent Me as long as it is day; night is coming when no one can work."

Another example John saw was the commission of the 72 disciples (Luke 10:2–3). Jesus told them, "the harvest is plentiful, but the workers are few," emphasizing the urgency and scarcity of the opportunity to spread the gospel.

The longer the community center took, the less opportunity people, especially the kids, would have to partake in all the good it could do. John knew he needed to use this principle to create a sense of urgency to complete the project as quickly as possible.

Unity. Of all the principles, unity was the one that struck John the deepest. Jesus's prayer in John 17:21 came to life, "That they may all be one, just as You, Father, are in Me, and I in You." It was a plea for connection that transcended normal human boundaries. Unity wasn't just about shared goals or common interests—it was a reflection of divine love.

Nehemiah led the Israelites in rebuilding Jerusalem's walls in just 52 days. That happened because they worked together with a singular purpose (Nehemiah 4:6). Their unity under a shared vision made the impossible possible. John had experienced this often as CEO at MediTech.

When the community center fostered unity, it would point people to God's kingdom, where every person belonged, without having to preach a sermon. Positioned well, unity would allay fears of proselytizing that might be a concern for those outside the church.

As he thought about this he wrote, "Community—come together in unity."

John closed his notebook, feeling a greater sense of purpose and clarity. It was as if he finally noticed something that had been there all along, like a beautiful sunrise or sunset, but now had a new appreciation for. These weren't just tools for sales or leadership—they were God-given truths about how people connect, grow, and love. If he led with these principles anchored in grace, the community center wouldn't just serve people—it would reflect the Kingdom.

As he contemplated on all he was learning, he bowed his head and prayed, "Lord, help me to fuse Your words with my understanding of influence. Help me lead this project with humility and love, so every principle I apply ultimately points people to You."

Reflection: True influence begins with the heart—and when guided by God's truth, it becomes a force for love, unity, and transformation. Like John, we're called to use what we've been given—skills, experience, insight—not just for our own purposes, but also to point others to Christ. Biblical influence isn't about control; it's about service grounded in truth. When we lead with humility and love, every interaction can become a reflection of Christ.

Chapter 7 – Jonathan and David

"The soul of Jonathan was knit to the soul of David, and Jonathan loved him as himself."

—*Samuel 18:1*

After John accepted the assignment, Dennis said he'd like to introduce him to Dave Sargent. The three planned to meet for coffee on Saturday morning for caffeine and conversation. The coffee shop buzzed with morning energy when John arrived around 7:45. The aroma of freshly ground beans mingled with the scent of warm pastries reminded him of Monday mornings long ago, meeting Duane—his business coach—in Dallas. Those coffee conversations had helped to shape his career and life. He hoped meeting Dave might be just as impactful.

John got his coffee and casually made his way to an open booth. The old leather crackled as he sat down. Within a few minutes, Dennis entered, and John waved him over to the booth.

After some casual conversation Dennis began to tell John about Dave's role in the community center. "Dave and Beth have been part of the congregation almost since the inception of The Rock. He's been an elder for nearly 15 years now. I asked him to oversee the project on behalf of the church because, as you're starting to find out, I'm not always easy to reach. With a growing church, I'm pulled in lots of different directions, so I need trusted people—those who share my vision and values—to help with big decisions."

John understood completely. "I get it, Dennis. By the time I left

Chapter 7 – Jonathan and David

MediTech, it had grown to twice the size it was when I stepped into the CEO role. Expansion like that necessitated having trusted, like-minded people to step in when I was unavailable. For me, Braedon Stanton was one such individual."

Dennis asked, "What made him such a trusted person for you?"

John then shared, "After Braedon opened up about his daughter's leukemia, we became close. When he discovered our CEO's ongoing embezzlement, we forged an even closer relationship. It was a scary time because we knew we could lose our jobs if we didn't handle the situation the right way. I respected Braedon for his integrity and courage through that ordeal. Eventually, he became the Senior Vice President of Finance for the company. I had complete confidence that Braedon would always make the right call in my absence."

"That's great John. As I said, I feel the same about Dave," Dennis told him.

John was familiar with Dave because of his position in the church but had never met him. Dave was a few years older than John and exuded confidence with everyone he met. After serving in the army right out of high school, he had moved to Clairemont and opened a thriving printing shop. He had some rough edges from his years in the armed forces, but those had softened considerably over time, and he enjoyed a good reputation inside and outside the church. He was always prompt and efficient, and he treated everyone fairly.

True to form, Dave walked in punctually at 8 a.m. He smiled and waved to Dennis and John as he stood in line to get his drink. It was obvious Dave had a military background. Some people entered a room unnoticed—Dave was not one of them. His posture was straight, eyes alert, as if still on duty. Every handshake came with direct eye contact and a sense of presence. John had dealt with countless leaders during his career but sensed there was something unique about Dave.

As Dave made his way to the table, John stood up, stepped forth and extended his hand. Dave met it with a firm grip. "Pleasure to finally meet you, John. I've known Abigail for several years because of her friendship with Beth and her involvement in outreach projects at the church. The way she speaks about you, I'd think Peter wasn't the only one who walked on water," he joked.

It always made John feel good when he knew Abigail spoke so highly of him to others. Of course, he always did the same when it came to her.

"Likewise, Dave. I feel like I know you a little because I've heard many great things about you from Abigail and Dennis. While I've been at the church for quite a few years, my career limited my participation. That's all behind me now, so I look forward to this next phase of life, and in particular, helping with the community center."

Once there was a pause, Dennis jumped in, "I've filled both of you in about each other and the community project, but I knew you had not formally met before, so I thought it was time we change that."

Dennis could sense an immediate bond between the two men. It reminded him of the deep friendship King David enjoyed with Jonathan, Saul's son. He felt John and Dave's connection was more than just camaraderie—it was a God-ordained friendship, built on a shared sense of purpose around the community center and loyalty to the church. He prayed this partnership would be just as strong. He decided to sit back and enjoy the conversation as it unfolded.

True to form, John took the lead, "Dave, I know about your involvement at the church and your printing business here in town, but I'd like to know more about you as a person. Tell me about your family and what brought you to Clairemont."

John had learned long ago that asking about family was a natural way to engage liking. It showed his genuine interest and made it easy for people to open up to him.

Dave shared that he'd married Beth, his high school sweetheart, shortly after graduation. He served 22 years in the army, which had them living in different parts of the country and included a few overseas assignments. By the time he retired, he'd risen to the rank of major and was in line for a promotion to colonel. As tempting as that next step was, he felt he'd given enough of himself to his country.

Like John and Abigail, Dave and Beth had two children, but theirs were both girls. They were now grandparents to three children, two boys and a newborn baby girl. He said he enjoyed fitness in his spare time, which was evident from his handshake and build.

As the conversation unfolded, they discovered more things in common; food, travel, sports, and a passion for helping people to grow professionally and personally.

"What's been your favorite place to travel to, Dave?" John asked.

"Italy for sure," Dave responded. "Beth and I went there for our 30th anniversary, and it was magical—the food, wine, and sights made for a romantic two-week vacation."

John could see the delight in Dave's face as he recounted the trip. "I hear you. We were there a few years ago. I think Abigail booked every tour there was in Rome. The highlight was Vatican City. Just contemplating the history in that place left me in awe," John shared.

Dave then asked John about his career. After sharing a bit about his journey, Dave said with the voice of a superior officer, "John, your career is impressive. However, I've got to be honest and say, much of what helped you in your corporate life might actually work against you in the church environment. I share that because my military background hasn't proved as helpful as I thought it might."

After a brief pause, his fingers tapping lightly on the edge of his coffee cup, Dave went on, "Yeah, the military taught me about discipline, but sometimes church feels like a whole different world—especially when dealing with people. It's not as clear-cut as the army. Sometimes I feel like I'm still figuring out where I fit in, even after all these years."

John knew there was a big difference between the command and control approach Dave had been a part of in the military and John's experience at MediTech. But he believed the more he combined scriptural principles with his understanding of influence, the less resistance he might face. Nonetheless, he graciously replied, "I appreciate you sharing that insight, Dave. I've no doubt there's lots more I can learn from you and your experience as a leader at The Rock."

Dennis was beaming as the conversation came to a close. As he'd hoped, John and Dave formed an immediate friendship that he believed would transcend their working together. This is what he'd been praying for. He knew John needed a partner on this project—someone with Dave's steadiness. He also knew Dave could benefit from John's relational approach to people and situations. However, he wasn't naïve, and he knew that even the strongest friendships could be tested by the pressures of leadership.

After about 45 minutes, Dave excused himself, telling Dennis and John that he and Beth were on grandparent duty soon, which entailed lunch and a movie with the little ones. "Beth has always been the steady one," Dave said. "She's the general who keeps our family running. I'm just along for the ride these days." John sensed some sarcasm in that remark.

"Yup, movies and babysitting the grandkids are what marriage is all about these days," Dave said with a chuckle.

John smiled but noticed Dave's expression didn't quite match his tone. There was a flicker in Dave's eyes—a shadow of something left unsaid. Before John could say anything more, Dave was already standing, his chair scraping the tile floor as he readied himself to leave.

John and Dennis remained at the coffee shop for another 15 minutes. John said, "I appreciate the introduction to Dave. I can tell we have quite a bit in common. I really look forward to working with him."

"He's a good man, disciplined and motivated. If you ask him to do anything, I guarantee he will exceed your expectations." Dennis knew that to be the case based on their long history together.

While they shared much in common, they'd taken very different paths to get to where they were so John knew he had much more to learn from Dave. He hoped he could help Dave learn from his experiences leading people in the business world.

John and Dennis dropped off their coffee mugs, made their way to the parking lot, and said their goodbyes.

Reflection: God often brings people together not because they are alike, but because their differences can serve a greater purpose. As was the case with Jonathan and David, true spiritual bonds are forged in trust, loyalty, and shared vision. John and

Dave's meeting was more than a partnership—it was a divine appointment. In your own life, who might God be calling you to walk alongside, not just to complete a project, but for something eternal?

Chapter 8 – Rebuilding the Walls

"Now it came about that when Sanballat heard that we were rebuilding the wall, he became furious and very angry and mocked the Jews."

—Nehemiah 4:1

John began to meet regularly with Dave to develop the mission and values that would guide the community center. Dennis had the vision, but he was humble enough to know he couldn't bring it to life alone. Big picture thinking came naturally to him, but drilling down into the details was not his strength. Fortunately, The Rock had many gifted members, and Dennis believed John and Dave were the right men to turn vision into reality.

In addition to talking about the community center, John and Dave chatted about life, faith, and marriage. One morning over coffee, John asked, "So how are you and Beth adjusting to grandparent life?"

Dave sighed and told him, "Beth and I are fine, but marriage at this stage of life? It's less fireworks and more … just knowing someone's always there. Sometimes I get a little nostalgic for the good old days when there was more passion and less routine."

John's mind went back to the 30th anniversary vacation Dave had talked about when they first met at the coffee shop. John remembered the twinkle in Dave's eye when he spoke of their anniversary trip to Italy—a spark now absent as Dave spoke of routine and nostalgia. "I hear you, Dave. After kids and decades of marriage, relationships are

Chapter 8 – Rebuilding the Walls

very different. Abigail and I have experienced some of the same things you describe, even though we're not grandparents yet."

"Do you ever long for the good old days," Dave asked.

"Yes and no," John replied. As he told Dave about the day he'd first laid eyes on Abigail at the gym as they ran side by side on treadmills, he could almost feel what it was like. He enjoyed those moments where he could feel those old sensations. He went on, "While intense feelings like that were wonderful, they don't last for anyone, and I wouldn't trade where we are now for anything. The love we feel now is deeper and there's a contentment to it."

"I guess you're right," Dave said with some resignation in his voice. He was hoping he might hear something different, something that gave a glimmer of hope.

After a brief pause, Dave cleared his throat. "Enough of that. Let's get to work." At that, his demeanor changed, and he was suddenly full of energy and ready to dive into the job at hand.

Regarding the community center, John and Dave developed a two-pronged approach they called, "Community and Congregation." Before the construction could start, they had to win over certain individuals and groups in the local community. But they didn't want to wait for city approval before approaching people in the congregation because once they got the green light, they wanted to hit the ground running. Success in both the corporate and military worlds required planning and parallel preparation—something both men understood well and excelled at.

To underscore urgency, John shared a verse that had stayed with him, "We must work the works of Him who sent Me as long as it is day" (John 9:4). Dave didn't need convincing—the mission was clear.

As they discussed their ideas, Dave brought up the story of Nehemiah. "John, are you familiar with Nehemiah from the Old Testament?" he asked.

John responded, "I am. Why?"

Dave began to share, "Nehemiah had been exiled in Babylon along with most of the Jews after the destruction of Solomon's temple. One day he felt the call of God to go back to Jerusalem to rebuild the walls and restore the Jewish community in the ancient city. Although God was involved, Nehemiah faced stiff opposition from the non-Jewish population in the surrounding area as well as some internal opposition from his own people."

"I see where you're going with this, Dave," John quickly replied.

"You know, Nehemiah didn't just pray and wait. He surveyed the walls at night, made strategic plans, and assigned specific tasks to certain people," Dave said. "Despite all the opposition he faced, Nehemiah was able to finish the rebuilding in just 52 days!"

On a smaller scale, Nehemiah's story mirrored what John and Dave would face—opposition from within and without. Nehemiah became their model for leadership and perseverance.

The people outside the church had to embrace the vision for the community center if it was to come into existence. They were going to need the approval of the city council before interacting with the zoning board. Two people would be key to gaining approval: Thomas May and Victoria Sparks.

Like many politicians, Thomas was a cautious man, always calculating public opinion. He'd lived in Clairemont since he was a young adult and enjoyed the prestige that came with being a councilman, a role he'd served in for nearly two decades. In his early 50s, Thomas had aspirations of becoming mayor in the next election, which was two years out. He knew projects that were readily adopted by the community would bolster his image and increase his chances of achieving that goal. In a very real sense, he was like the doubting Thomas of the Bible; he needed to see to believe. John knew he'd have to paint a vivid picture of what the community center would look like once it was operational and how it would benefit everyone in Clairemont.

Victoria Sparks was a different story. A life-long Clairemont resident, she was outspoken and fiercely independent. She viewed anything remotely religious with suspicion because of childhood wounds that had never quite healed. In her view, the church was full of hypocrites, so she wanted nothing to do with it.

Victoria was on the city council and was also an active school board

Chapter 8 – Rebuilding the Walls

member. She'd earned quite a reputation for being vocal about her views. People joked that her name fit her well because when issues came before the city council or school board, quite often sparks flew! Not only did she adamantly oppose anything religious in the school system, no matter how ecumenical, but she also held a similar view when it came to community projects. Much of her opposition was fueled by her childhood experience and by sheer force of will; more often than not, she was victorious. A staunch supporter of the separation of church and state, several times over the years it was her deciding vote that prevented various religious organizations from utilizing school resources in any way, even after regular school hours. Although the community center was entirely separate from the school system, it would be heavily geared towards kids, so John and Dave anticipated strong opposition from Victoria. She was their Sanballat, and they knew it.

John said, "Both might be tough to win over, but it's essential we get at least one on our side quickly because if we do so, it will be much easier to win over others thereafter. Who do you recommend we start with?"

"Thomas, of course," Dave replied. That's what John thought but he also knew it was important to get Dave's buy-in. John nodded. Hearing Dave say it out loud affirmed what he'd already believed. It was a subtle use of consistency—when people commit verbally, they're more likely to follow through.

Dave went on, "He's the better person to focus on, at least to start, because of his tenure, standing in the community, and the fact that he's less opposed to projects that have some religious connection."

After further discussion they moved on to the church, a different challenge but a very real one, nonetheless. Raising funds and soothing certain people would be the main obstacles. The local economy wasn't doing well, and, as Abigail had shared with Dennis and John weeks earlier, many in the congregation were exhausted by the number of projects over the years that required contributions above and beyond normal giving.

Dave went first, "The biggest obstacle might be Martha Cook." She was a respected, long-time member of the church. She'd enjoyed a successful career in IT project management before retiring a few years earlier. While she was initially excited about the vision Dennis laid out, Dave told John, "She's hurt that she wasn't approached for the role that went to you, John. She's let more than a few church members know that."

John felt a twinge in his gut at that news, but it wasn't the first time he'd encountered a situation like this. "I get it, Dave. When I was tapped to be CEO at MediTech I was pretty young, and several more seasoned leaders resented it. I was able to win most over, but a couple couldn't deal with it and left within a year."

Like Abigail, Martha served in many volunteer capacities. Between that and her project management background, she felt like she'd earned the right to take on a big project like the community center. "I just don't understand why they didn't ask me," Martha said to a friend after church. "I've managed projects larger than this community center. I'm not bitter—it's just disappointing." In reality, a root of bitterness was growing inside her and her comments were not helping the community center project.

Those conversations have a way of making the rounds, whether in a church or a business, and Dave and John eventually caught wind of it. They knew workers like Martha were essential to make church projects a success. It would be important to win her over as soon as possible so her words wouldn't negatively influence others in the congregation.

"Dave, I'll talk with Martha. I think it's important that she hear from me because I wouldn't want her to think I was avoiding her or trying to cut her out of the project."

"I think that's wise. I've always believed the direct approach is the best route to victory," Dave responded, using a military example in the same way that many use sports analogies.

As John walked to his car, he felt the weight of the project settle onto his shoulders. This was more than just building a community center—it was about healing wounds in people like Victoria and Martha. It was also a chance to build bridges in the community and demonstrate the love of Christ in a tangible way. He took a deep breath, closed his eyes, and whispered, "Lord, guide our steps. Give me the wisdom to lead well and the humility to listen."

Chapter 8 – Rebuilding the Walls

Reflection: Every work of God encounters opposition—sometimes from without, sometimes from within. Like Nehemiah, we're called not only to build, but also to stand firm when others mock or resist. John and Dave's mission reminds us that faithful leadership requires courage, strategy, and unity. What walls in your life—or community—might God be calling you to rebuild?

Chapter 9 – Don't Hinder the Children

"Permit the children to come to Me, and do not hinder them, for the kingdom of God belongs to such as these."

—Luke 18:16

John knew that Dave had a loose relationship with Thomas. They didn't run in the same social circles, but they were more than acquaintances because, being a business owner in town, Dave had dealt with Thomas on many occasions. Rather than cold calling Thomas, John asked Dave if he would reach out on his behalf. He'd used a similar approach when he was in sales and almost every time he got a warm introduction, it led to an in-person meeting.

John approached Dave with the idea, "Would you be open to introducing me to Thomas? I ask because during my career I've seen this approach work far better than picking up the phone and making a cold call."

Although Dave had run his print shop for quite a while, he wasn't as business savvy as John because John's background was more varied having been in sales, run the MediTech corporate university, and spent time as a senior executive. John knew a warm introduction from Dave would allow him to leverage authority—Dave could share about John in a way that, coming from John himself, might sound boastful. "Seems like a good approach," Dave replied.

"Thanks. I don't want this to be a burden, so how about I give you something you can use to make the introduction?" John asked.

The offer was a welcomed relief for Dave because writing wasn't his strong suit. Together they tweaked John's intro, and Dave sent the email that afternoon. Despite his busy schedule, Thomas replied before the end of the day, asking that John call him so they could look at their schedules and get something on the calendar. John called the next morning, and they scheduled lunch for the following Wednesday. During the call, Thomas was clear that they'd each pick up their own tab so there was no hint of quid pro quo.

***

As was his custom, John arrived 10 minutes early at Mancini's, a nice Italian restaurant in the uptown area of Clairemont. He and Abigail had eaten there many times, so John got to know Domonic Mancini, the owner. The restaurant had been a Clairemont staple for three decades, its red-and-white checkered tablecloths and old black-and-white photos of Italy gave it a cozy, authentic Italian feel. Even more important than the atmosphere, the food was excellent! Upon entering, John saw Domonic and the two shook hands.

It was a little before noon, but the restaurant was filling quickly. The clatter of silverware and the hum of conversations filled the space. A waiter passed by with a steaming plate of pasta, and the aroma of marinara and fresh basil lingered in the air, turning heads as the waiter passed.

"What brings you in today, John," Domonic asked.

"I'm meeting Thomas May. The Rock wants to build a community center, and I'd like to share the vision with him."

"Sounds like something the city could really benefit from," Domonic excitedly said.

"I hope Thomas shares your enthusiasm, Domonic," John replied with a smile.

The two continued chatting when Thomas walked in. John noticed Thomas greeting people by name, stopping to shake hands, exchange smiles—a man deeply rooted in the community. He knew all the business owners in town, so he enthusiastically waved to Domonic as he walked over to him and John. Domonic took the lead and said, "Thomas, good to see you. John was sharing some news with me that you'll be very interested in."

It was almost as if John got an unpaid testimonial. Smiling, he shook Thomas's hand and said, "So nice to finally meet you, Thomas. I appreciate all you and the council do for Clairemont. Abigail and I love living here." At that point Domonic guided them to a table in the back of the restaurant so they could have some privacy.

As they sat down Thomas said, "Dave speaks highly of you, John. He has a great reputation in town so anyone he recommends meeting is worth getting to know."

A young mother approached their table with her little boy. "Excuse me Councilman May, I just wanted to say thank you for getting that crosswalk put in near the school. It's made such a difference."

Thomas smiled, his demeanor shifting. "Just doing my part, Amanda. Glad to see you and little Ethan out and about. Tell Fred I said hello."

John could see how much that short interaction meant to Thomas. He was more than a politician; he was a genuine man who wanted to help the residents of Clairemont.

After a few more pleasantries, they placed their orders, and the waiter took their menus. It was at that point that John began to share the vision for the community center. He could see that Thomas was listening intently and critically thinking, absorbing everything John was saying.

"John, I like what you're sharing but I have to be honest, having a church expand in such a way is going to be met with some resistance, particularly from Victoria. If this were privately funded instead of by the church, I doubt anyone would have issue with it," Thomas stated matter-of-factly.

Thomas hadn't always been so cautious. Early in his career, he'd championed a playground project that ultimately failed, costing the city tens of thousands of dollars. Now the plot of land sat empty. For a small town, that was huge, and the backlash was swift, nearly derailing his political ambitions. Since then, he had learned to weigh every decision carefully, prioritizing his career over taking risks.

Chapter 9 – Don't Hinder the Children

Having to sell his ideas was nothing new to John, so he'd anticipated this particular concern and Victoria's opposition. He resorted to a time-tested sales approach, "I understand your concern Thomas because others have expressed similar concerns." Then, to shift the focus he went on, "However, I'd like you to consider this. In reality, the community center will be privately funded. The citizens of Clairemont who happen to be members of the church would be the ones voluntarily donating the money." It was an interesting way to reframe the issue. John watched as Thomas's eyebrows lifted—he'd struck a chord.

John let Thomas mull it over for a few seconds then went on, "No individual in this community could pull this off by themselves. It just so happens that many people in the church see the good it could do for the town so we'd like to see if we can make it happen. In addition to the church, we've had several business owners express interest in the project. They see the potential not just for their families but for the entire community."

"That's good to know," Thomas replied. "I've seen good projects fail because they didn't consider the political landscape. You know who else has to come on board, don't you?"

John smiled—Thomas had just lobbed him a softball. "I understand Victoria might oppose the project so, because of your tenure and standing in the community, we decided to approach you with the idea first. If you're on board, it will be more likely that others on the council will follow your lead. Without your support, we know it's unlikely we'll get the votes we need. If that happens, it would be a shame because it's the kids who will lose out."

John knew appealing to Thomas's reputation with the council meant a lot to him because he was the longest standing member. But it was the mention of the kids that struck a deeper chord—John saw it in the softening of Thomas's eyes, similar to his earlier response to the young mother and her son. John's research had let him know that Thomas was the grandfather of six, all under the age of 12. Each of them would benefit from the community center for years to come.

"You mentioned the kids, John," Thomas said, his voice softening. "What kind of programs are you thinking about?"

"We'd love to offer after-school tutoring, sports, crafts, and maybe even a mentorship program," John said. "We believe a safe place can change kids' trajectories. It's about more than keeping them busy—it's about giving them support and hope."

"You know, I've had proposals come across my desk before, but they were mostly about the business side—how it would help the economy, boost tourism, etc. You're talking about the kids. That's different," Thomas said.

Rather than thinking about why it might not work, John could see Thomas was beginning to think about how it *could* work. He wasn't looking to close the deal at this time, but moving Thomas in his direction would be a big first step.

As Thomas spoke, John did some quick mental accounting of the influence principles. Liking, authority, social proof, and scarcity—he'd already woven each into the conversation. Now, it was time to reinforce consistency. If he could get Thomas to voice even a small commitment, it would set the stage for a stronger agreement in the future.

John leaned into consistency. "I'm not looking for a yes today," he said, giving Thomas room to reflect while planting the seed for a future commitment. "This is a big deal and I'm sure you'll have other concerns to consider as you talk with other council members. I would like to ask this; would you give it thought and be willing to meet next week to discuss it further?"

Thomas agreed that was reasonable, so they checked their calendars and decided to meet for coffee the following Tuesday to resume their conversation.

As they finished their meals Thomas said, "John, thanks for reaching out and asking for my input. I need to get to an afternoon meeting, but I look forward to speaking again next week."

As John was about to exit Domonic asked, "How did it go, John?"

"Excellent, Domonic! Thomas is interested and agreed to float the idea to some of the other council members. We're going to meet again next week to resume the conversation."

"That's great news! Best of luck," Domonic said as John paid his bill.

Chapter 9 – Don't Hinder the Children

Sitting in his car, John replayed the conversation in his mind. He felt good about the meeting, but he knew better than to celebrate prematurely. He pulled out his notebook and jotted down key points—what had resonated with Thomas, what questions had gone unanswered, and what concerns might come up the following week. Preparation, John knew, wasn't just about success—it was about stewardship. He was advocating for something bigger than himself. He could hardly wait to share with Abigail and Dave how things had unfolded with Thomas.

> **Reflection:** When we advocate for what truly matters—especially for those who may not be able to speak up for themselves, like children—God calls us to lead with wisdom, love, and courage. John's meeting with Thomas reminds us that influence, when guided by service and truth, can open doors that might otherwise remain closed. Who in your life needs you to speak up—not for your own gain, but for their good? Influence isn't about winning arguments; it's about advancing God's Kingdom one conversation, one relationship, at a time.

Chapter 10 – Trouble Brewing

*"In the world you have tribulation,
but take courage; I have overcome the world"*

—John 16:33

While John felt encouraged by his meeting with Thomas, trouble was already brewing—Victoria had caught wind of the community center plans. She also knew John had just met with Thomas. It bothered her to think John was working around her to garner wider support. Truthfully, that *was* John's strategy—but nothing unethical. Years in sales and leadership had taught him the value of gaining advocates early. He also reasoned that Jesus used a similar approach when He called the 12 apostles and worked extensively with them before making his ministry more public.

As John pondered Christ's approach, he realized another time Jesus had used a principle of influence. Before Jesus called Peter and Andrew, He told them to push out their boat and cast their nets. After a short protest—they'd fished all night but caught nothing—they agreed. Suddenly their nets were so full the boat nearly sank! Jesus had engaged reciprocity—giving them a miraculous catch, something that mattered deeply to fishermen, before inviting them to follow Him and become fishers of men.

Her bruised ego made Victoria dig in on her opposition to the community center and she began to make it known in subtle and not so subtle ways. Victoria's subtle tactic? Initiating "casual" conversations

Chapter 10 – Trouble Brewing

with council members she believed she could sway. She made sure to do this quickly, hoping to reach them before Thomas or John had an opportunity to do so. She conveyed her feelings under the guise of what was best for the kids and how religion, while "fine for individuals," should be confined to the church and individual's personal beliefs.

"I hear The Rock wants to build a community center," she told one council member. "I think it's a nice idea, but I'm not sure people want their kids hanging out at a place where there will be a heavy influence from the church. If they wanted that, I suppose they'd just go to church. Don't you agree?" The council member nodded as he listened to Victoria.

She went on, "If some parents are uncomfortable and don't want their kids there, those kids might feel ostracized not being with their friends."

She paused to let that thought settle. "I just don't know if this is the right direction for Clairemont. What happens if it starts as a community center and turns into a church outreach program?"

The council member continued nodding slowly. "My kids already feel enough pressure at school. I don't want them feeling it after hours, too."

"Exactly," Victoria said, her tone empathetic. "I just think we need to explore all our options before jumping into something this exclusive."

Her conversations were intended to sow seeds of doubt, and she was skillful at it. She knew she wasn't going to convince everyone, but she didn't need to. All she needed was a few voices of dissent to slow the project down. If she could create enough uncertainty, the votes might never materialize, and the project would die on the vine.

Her not-so-subtle maneuver was to approach Stan Letterman, who happened to be the editor of the local newspaper, the Clairemont Courier. Stan had taken over the newspaper when he moved to town several years before with his wife and children. He'd been an investigative reporter in Newark, NJ, but realized the unpredictable hours weren't conducive to raising a family. He and his wife felt the pace of a small town like Clairemont would be best for them. Because of his role as editor, he had a chance to meet most of the prominent people in town.

Always one to have his pulse on the happenings in Clairemont, Stan heard rumblings about the community center project and thought it might make a good story for the paper in the coming weeks. Victoria was delighted to hear that and shared more of her views, hoping he would publish a story that would slant readers to her way of thinking. What she didn't count on was Stan's integrity—as a fair-minded reporter, he insisted on hearing both sides.

"Stan, I'm just not sure this is what the community needs," Victoria said, her voice measured but firm.

"What makes you say that?" Stan asked, leaning back in his chair, pen poised above his notepad.

"A church-run community center sounds good on paper, but you know how these things go. It starts with games and after-school programs, but before you know it, kids are being pressured into faith-based activities."

Stan tapped his pen thoughtfully. "But if it's voluntary, is that still a problem?"

"Parents might feel they don't have a choice if their kids have friends who go there. Kids always want to be with their friends," Victoria replied. "We need options that are truly neutral, not tied to any religious agenda."

After she left, Stan picked up the phone to get input directly from Dennis.

"Dennis, I just spoke to Victoria Sparks. She has some pretty definite views about your community center project. Care to share your side of things?" Stan asked. He always got directly to the point. In that regard he was like Sgt. Joe Friday from the old television show, Dragnet, who was famous for routinely saying, "Just the facts."

Dennis briefly shared his vision then Stan said, "You and I know Victoria has concerns. She's pretty vocal about keeping church and community separate."

"I respect her perspective," Dennis replied. "We're not looking to force anything on anyone. The community center isn't about conversion—it's about creation, creating a safe space for kids. If faith comes up, it will happen because kids ask questions in the course of normal conversation, not because of recruitment."

Chapter 10 – Trouble Brewing

"What about parents who are wary of religious influence?" Stan asked.

"That's a fair question. We plan to involve community leaders from different backgrounds. We want this to be a place where everyone feels welcome, regardless of their beliefs."

Dennis could tell Stan was taking notes, so he went on, "You know how busy I am Stan, so I'm not in on all of the day-to-day decisions around the community center. Dave Sargent, because of his many years as an elder, is taking the lead on this for me. But it's really John Andrews you want to speak with. Knowing his years of successfully running MediTech, I felt he was the best person to shepherd this project." Stan thanked Dennis and said he would reach out to John.

***

Call it good luck or divine intervention, fortunately for John, Stan called him early on Monday, the day before his next meeting with Thomas.

Stan started the call, "John, I spoke to Dennis about his community center idea. He suggested I reach out to you because he said you're the man who will make the vision a reality."

Before Stan could go on, John interjected, "I'm flattered that he said that Stan but let me set the record straight. I'm going to play an important role but nothing great in life or business happens because of one person. It takes a team and once we get the green light from the city, Dave Sargent and I will assemble a talented group of people from the church, and outside of it, to bring the community center into existence."

Stan was taken back a bit because of John's humility. He'd interviewed plenty of politicians and executives—humility, in his experience, was rare.

As they continued to talk, Stan said, "I have to tell you, there are some people who are opposed to the project." He shared some details without mentioning Victoria by name, but John instinctively knew who Stan was referring to. John felt a tinge of frustration—Victoria's vocal opposition was based on personal feelings, not facts—but he remained calm, determined to lead with grace.

Never one to lose his composure, John calmly addressed the issue, "Good things in life and business never come easy Stan because there are always people who see things differently. Sometimes their reasons are valid and sometimes not. We want to address any concerns, so people are comfortable with the project. However, I've also seen over the course of my career, there are always some who won't change their views, no matter how well their concerns are addressed."

He paused before continuing. "Our goal is simple: to do the most good for the most people—and we believe the community center will do just that."

"John, some people are worried the community center will be more about promoting the church than serving the kids," Stan said, not shying away from the tough question.

"I understand the concern, and I'd feel the same if I thought that was our goal," John said. "But our mission is simple—give kids a safe place to learn, play, and interact. We want parents to feel good about where their kids are spending time."

"But what about the faith component? Can you really keep that separate?" Stan pressed.

"We believe faith is shown through actions, not just words," John replied. "If kids ask questions, we'll answer honestly, but no one will be pressured. If the community center isn't a place where all feel welcome, then we've missed the mark."

John's answers were thoughtful and clear. He wasn't defensive or dismissive—he seemed genuinely invested in making the project about the community, not the church.

He paused momentarily, then asked Stan, "I understand you have children. Don't you think your kids would love a place to be with their friends—to play, have fun, and just be kids?" He intentionally made it more personal for Stan by saying "your kids."

Softening a bit, Stan replied, "I know they would, John. A community center has a lot of appeal for kids and parents. The kids don't have the pressure of schoolwork and parents would benefit knowing their kids are in a safe place."

John was smiling because the more Stan spoke, just as was the case with Thomas, the more he would convince himself that the center would be a good thing for the town and surrounding communities. As Dale Carnegie, author of *How to Win Friends and Influence People*, wrote, "Let the other person feel the idea is theirs." John smiled, knowing that principle would shape Stan's next article.

After hanging up, still sitting at his desk, Stan reviewed his notes. Victoria's concerns were valid, but Dennis and John had offered thoughtful, direct answers. He decided to write a draft that included both perspectives. He wanted readers to make up their own minds, but he also felt a responsibility to present the facts without bias. Balancing perspectives was never easy—but Stan knew that true journalism didn't demand neutrality; it demanded fairness.

> **Reflection:** Faithful leadership will always face resistance—sometimes from misunderstanding, sometimes from fear. Like John, we're called to respond not with defensiveness, but with grace, humility, and truth. When opposition arises, are you prepared to lead with calm conviction? As Jesus reminded us, "In the world, you will have tribulation, but take courage; I have overcome the world" (John 16:33). Kingdom work isn't easy—but it's always worth it.

Chapter 11 – An Influential Article

*"No weapon that is formed against you will prosper;
And every tongue that accuses you in judgment you will condemn."*

—Isaiah 54:17

John met with Thomas the next day at The Coffee House, a local shop that had thrived despite a Starbucks opening down the street several years earlier. It was the kind of place where baristas knew your name and your order—familiar, warm, and unmistakably local.

The meeting was productive, but Thomas still expressed some doubt and shared a few new concerns raised by the council members he'd spoken with.

"John, I'll be candid," Thomas said, stirring his coffee. "Some of the council members are worried that this community center might blur the line between church and state."

"I understand the concern," John replied, "but I don't see it as a church and state issue. The city isn't promoting the church any more than when it gave approval for us to build The Rock. That aside, we've been careful to design this as a true community space. Yes, members of the church will be funding it, but it will be open to everyone—no strings attached."

"But what about concerns that kids will feel pressured to join the church?" Thomas asked.

John felt like a broken record, but he knew Thomas wasn't just challenging him—he was seeking reassurance, weighing trust. Influence

Chapter 11 – An Influential Article

wasn't about winning a debate; it was about building relationships and trust with transparency.

"That's not our intent," John said. He leaned forward, looking Thomas directly in the eye, "We want kids to feel safe and accepted, regardless of their beliefs. If faith comes up, it will be through natural conversation, just as it might occur anywhere, but not through organized programs." Drawing on social proof, John added, "Our research indicates this approach has worked in other towns, and it strengthens communities because it brings people from all walks of life together."

More questions came and, after skillfully addressing each one, knowing Thomas needed to "see to believe," John began to paint a picture of a bustling community center, and what he believed would be the response from children and parents.

"Thomas, imagine school letting out and kids making their way to the community center. They're excited because for an hour or two, they can let the cares of the day go. They run inside and see familiar volunteers who greet them by name and ask about their day. Some kids are shooting hoops while others are engaged in various activities. Later, parents come to pick up their children who excitedly run up to them and show a piece of art they created or a story they wrote. Doesn't that sound like something every family in Clairemont could benefit from?"

How could Thomas say no? The more John went on, the more Thomas's doubts receded.

Then, unprompted, Thomas suggested, "Would you, Dennis, and Dave be willing to address the city council at our next meeting? It's open to the public and takes place in two weeks."

That would give the trio plenty of time to decide on the best approach to address the council and questions from residents of Clairemont so John replied, "That would be great, Thomas."

Thomas opened his day planner to jot down a few notes. As he did so, John said, "Thomas, I'm glad you're feeling more comfortable with the project. Before that meeting, I'd like to ask for a favor."

Thomas inquired, "Depends on what it is." As a politician, he was used to people asking for favors, so he always had his guard up.

"Fair enough," John said with a smile. "I know the newspaper is going to run an article on the community center proposal this Friday. Would you be willing to have conversations with some of the members before the next council meeting to address their concerns now that we've talked? I ask because I believe that will help us have a more productive conversation with them at the council meeting." John deliberately used "because"—he'd learned long ago that giving a reason using that specific word often turned a maybe into a yes.

"I communicate with most of them multiple times a week so I can certainly do that," Thomas responded confidently.

Between the sway Thomas held in the community and the upcoming article, John was starting to feel better about the prospects of getting approval from the city. The positive views Thomas now held would pre-suade many in the community and on the council, making it easier to get the approval they needed.

***

True to his word, Stan published the article in the Friday edition of the paper. The Clairemont Courier was a typical small town newspaper, always looking for good stories that impacted residents, so it was the lead story above the fold. The headline read: *New Community Center Proposal: A Place for All*. The article opened with Dennis's vision of a safe space for children, highlighted community questions, then addressed Victoria's concerns. It concluded with John's thoughtful responses.

"John Andrews, former CEO of MediTech, emphasized that the center would be 'a welcoming place for all, regardless of faith or background.' He addressed concerns directly, stating, 'We want this center to be a resource for the entire community, not just an extension of The Rock.'"

Much to Victoria's dismay, the final section of the article felt like a rebuttal of her concerns. In reality, it was the fair thing to do. John knew her concerns and thoughtfully addressed each one in an attempt to begin to win over the town's residents.

Chapter 11 – An Influential Article

That Sunday, before starting his sermon, Dennis held up the paper, smiled, and told the congregation, "This is more than just a building project—it's an opportunity to live out our faith in a tangible way. Jesus said, 'Let the little children come to Me.' This center will be a place where kids can feel safe, loved, and valued."

He publicly thanked John and Dave for taking the lead on the project then singled out John for his thoughtful comments in the article. He encouraged everyone to pick up a copy of the paper to read the article in case neighbors asked about it.

Some in the congregation nodded in agreement, while others exchanged cautious glances. Dennis noticed the mixed reactions and addressed them directly. "I know some of you might be wondering what this means for us financially. I promise we'll approach this project with wisdom and transparency. Our goal is to serve, not to burden."

John noticed Martha—arms crossed, lips tight—fanning the flames of discontent, a clear sign that she still wasn't happy. She turned to the person next to her and whispered, "We just paid off the sanctuary remodel, and now we're starting something new? Why are we always being asked to give more?" It was a legitimate concern for many.

It took John and Abigail longer than usual to make their way out of the building because of the people who came up to John to thank him for his words in the newspaper. Much to John's delight, many said they'd like to volunteer when the city gave approval. No one said, "If the city approves"—they had faith the city would approve the project.

Despite the well-wishers, John knew not everyone shared the same sentiment. He overheard someone walking by, "I'm all for helping kids, but my wallet needs a break." Another person muttered, "If they start passing the plate for this, I'm out." These undercurrents of doubt made John realize there was much more groundwork to be laid. He'd not anticipated such a strong reaction from so many from within the church.

As they walked to their car, Abigail reached for John's hand. "You did great today," she said softly. "People are starting to see your heart for this project. Are you feeling a sense of purpose again?"

John had mixed emotions. "I am but did you hear what Martha said and some of the people walking by? There are still a lot of questions—and I get it. The last thing we want is for people to feel pressured. If we can't get support from within, we might be doomed."

Abigail nodded. "Maybe that's an opportunity to show people what this is really about. Not about money, but about ministry. We have to have faith."

That evening, as John sat on his porch alone with his thoughts, he opened his Bible to Isaiah 54:17. "No weapon that is formed against you will prosper; And every tongue that accuses you in judgment you will condemn." He whispered, "Lord, show me what to do. Give me wisdom to navigate what lies ahead."

Reflection: Influence doesn't guarantee smooth sailing—it often reveals unexpected resistance, especially from those we assume are already with us. Like John, we're reminded that Kingdom work begins with faith, not unanimous support. As Isaiah promises, no weapon formed against God's purpose will prevail. When voices rise in opposition, will you press on in faith and humility, trusting God to equip you for what's ahead?

Chapter 12 – Before the Judges

"But when they hand you over, do not worry about how or what you are to say; for it will be given you in that hour what you are to say. For it is not you who speak, but it is the Spirit of your Father who speaks in you."

—Matthew 10:19–20

In the week since the article had come out, John spent time preparing his remarks for the council meeting. He would be limited to five minutes, so he had to be concise. After he made his case, there would be time set aside for remarks from individuals in the community and questions from the council members.

Thursday afternoon John and Abigail were getting ready to attend the council meeting which would start at 6 p.m. and run for two hours. "Are you excited?" Abigail asked.

It didn't escape John's notice that she avoided the word "nervous." She'd learned from him long ago that excitement and nerves were often two sides of the same coin—what you labeled it could shape how you faced it.

Smiling he replied, "Very excited. It feels like the old days going before the board to get approval for a new strategic project. As important as those asks were, this one has consequences that are more far reaching."

John and Abigail arrived early and sat in the room in which public forums were held. John wanted to get comfortable with the venue beforehand since he'd never attended a council meeting. There were seven large chairs behind a raised, semi-circle table that allowed the council members to see one another. In front of the table was a podium with a mic for residents to address the council and allow those behind them to hear their remarks clearly.

About 15 minutes after John and Abigail arrived, people began to filter in. In Clairemont, city council meetings always drew a crowd but whenever a faith-based project was up for debate, the crowds were larger. Clairemont, nestled in the southern Bible belt, was filled with people of faith—but they didn't always agree on how faith should influence public life. Dave and Dennis took seats in the front row beside John and Abigail. Stan sat in the front row on the other side of the aisle so he could observe the reactions from council members. He looked at John, smiled and winked, as if to say, "Good luck." Much to their surprise, by the time the council members took their seats at five till six, the venue was completely full and had many people standing in the back and along the side walls.

Being the senior council member, Thomas May opened the meeting, and after the normal formalities, he set the stage for the community center project being proposed by The Rock. Then he asked John to come up to address the council. Never one to read prepared remarks, John just wrote a few bullet points so he would not forget anything important.

"Council members, thank you for giving me a few minutes to share about a very important project for our community. Before I get going, I want to acknowledge each of you for your efforts on behalf of our community. I know sometimes your job may seem thankless, but it's your efforts that make Clairemont a place so many of us enjoy. None more than my wife, Abigail, and me. We have loved our time here and so did our children before they moved on." John knew it was important to offer a sincere compliment to engage liking and reduce resistance.

"The project I'll talk about is on behalf of my church, The Rock. Dennis Reacher, our Senior Pastor has a vision for a community center that would be open to all residents, regardless of their beliefs, and without charge. The vision primarily centers around our children, to give them a safe space to laugh, play, and have the kind of fun children should enjoy. However, it's not only the children who will benefit. I know many parents struggle to make ends meet and quite often that means their children come home to an empty house because they're still at work. From the many conversations I've had over the last several weeks, I know those parents want a safe place their children can go after school. I can relate because years ago, when our kids were young, we worried about where they'd go after school. We were fortunate to find a place that provided a safe environment and helped them build lifelong friendships. Not every family has that option. This community center is our chance to fill that gap for parents and their kids."

As John spoke, he noticed one council member, a woman in her 40s, nodding slowly. Another, a younger man sitting to Victoria's left, scribbled notes furiously but didn't look up. Victoria herself sat rigid; her hands clasped tightly on the desk; her eyes fixed on John.

He went on to share the kinds of activities the children would have access to and how the community center would be staffed. He let the council know that anyone in the community could participate through giving or volunteering. It would truly be a "community" center for all of the residents.

After laying out the vision and painting a picture of what the community center would look like once it was operational, he continued, "I'd like to take my remaining time to address concerns the council may have as well as people who do not attend The Rock. First, there will be no religious instruction and no attempts to get anyone to attend our church or any other. Having said that, it will be an atmosphere where love and generosity are stressed. I doubt anyone would object to knowing attendees would be encouraged to love and respect others, that it's important to be a selfless giver, to always tell the truth, and to say sorry when they've done something wrong. Are any of these bad things?" He paused to give people an opportunity to answer the question for themselves. He could see several council members nodding in agreement, with one notable exception. Victoria had a scowl on her face that only grew worse when one person on the council looked at her as if to say, "He's right."

John went on, "I think those are very good things and we'd all benefit from children and adults alike, who embrace such ideals."

Victoria interrupted, "I've heard all of this before. Churches promise no pressure, but I've seen how it works. Kids are vulnerable, and I won't support any project that risks blurring the line between public good and private agenda."

"I respect your concerns, Victoria," John said. "We have no intention of proselytizing. We're offering a space, not a sermon. Our focus is simple: safety, education, and community support. The values we teach—love, respect, honesty—aren't religious—they're human."

He finished his prepared remarks, and he closed with, "It's our sincere hope that we can come to agreement tonight that our kids deserve a place like the community center. I look forward to addressing any other concerns you, or those in attendance, may have."

Applause erupted from many in the audience and Thomas had to ask people to please restrain themselves. One by one, people made their way to the podium to share.

"I'm a single mom," a young woman said. "I work two jobs, and I worry every day about where my kids go after school. A community center like this could be life-changing for families like mine."

The vast majority were in favor of the idea. The few that were against it usually had issue with the fact that it would come from the church. They didn't believe a church would do something like this without an ulterior motive.

"I get the idea," one man said. "But what happens if leadership changes at The Rock? What if this starts as a safe space and turns into something else?"

Next came comments from the council, so John made his way back to the podium so he could answer or clarify for each issue that came up. As he anticipated, Victoria continued to be the real challenge. She told everyone how important the children of Clairemont were to her and stressed, that's why she volunteered for the school board. People familiar with her believed she was more concerned about the power she exerted as part of the city council and school board than she was for the good of the children.

Chapter 12 – Before the Judges

John said with a tone of sincerity, "Victoria, we all appreciate your service. We need more people who are willing to be as involved in the community as you are. While I obviously don't hold the same view that you do regarding faith-based projects, you and I are in agreement on this; we both want what's best for the children in our community. We happen to have different views on how best to go about it. Unfortunately, no organization has stepped up to provide for this need so people in the community who happen to be members of the Rock feel compelled to provide a solution. Isn't that kind of community involvement a good thing?"

His words drew nods—even from those Victoria thought were firmly in her corner. She knew John was right and couldn't disagree that a community center could be beneficial. However, it's difficult for most people who've taken a public stance to recant, so she pressed further. That approach only worked against her.

John silently recalled Proverbs 15:1, "A gentle answer turns away wrath, but a harsh word stirs up anger." He maintained his tone, offering gentleness instead of rebuttal. He could see he was successful with the others but much like Pharoah when he interacted with Moses, Victoria continued to harden her heart.

The meeting was drawing to a close, so Thomas stepped into the fray. He'd been on the council longer than anyone, and like most long-serving politicians, he knew when to be cautious and when to push forward. Addressing the council members he said, "It's rare that the entire council agrees on everything. However, I think we've heard enough that we can take a vote."

Immediately Victoria said in an exasperated tone, "You're being manipulated by a well-crafted speech, Thomas. But let's be honest—if this weren't a church project, we wouldn't even be having this debate."

Unfazed, Thomas asked the council for a vote by a show of hands. As soon as he did so, two hands went up immediately, including Thomas's. After a pause that felt like an eternity, a third and fourth hand rose—then a fifth. The final two were members Victoria thought she had in her corner. Neither would look at her as they held their hands in the air. Only Victoria and a longtime ally of hers refrained from voting yes. With that Thomas gave approval for the project and advised John, Dave, and Dennis to reach out to the city zoning board to get the project under way.

As people came up to congratulate John he had mixed emotions. While grateful for the approval, John felt a heaviness—Victoria hadn't just lost a vote; she was carrying pain, and it showed. She grabbed her items, glaring in John's direction, and marched out the side door without a word to anyone. Her anger was evident to everyone in attendance. Knowing it's never good to have enemies, John decided he would do his best to smooth things over with Victoria, if that were possible.

> **Reflection:** Victory in leadership is not just about winning approval—it's about stewarding influence with grace and compassion, even toward those who oppose us. John's calm, respectful approach in the face of conflict reflects Christ's words, "Do not worry beforehand about what you are to say, but say whatever is given you in that hour; for it is not you who speak, but it is the Holy Spirit" (Mark 13:11). When facing resistance, will you speak with wisdom and humility, trusting God to work through you?

Chapter 13 – Martha, Martha

"Martha, Martha, you are worried and bothered about so many things; but only one thing is necessary."

—Luke 10:41–42

As he'd done weeks before, after the newspaper article appeared, Dennis shared the good news regarding the council meeting with the congregation the Sunday after the meeting. The response was generally positive but somewhat subdued, and Dennis could tell there was something he was missing. The congregation usually responded with energy to good news—but this time, the mood felt muted.

After the service Dennis asked Dave and John to join him for a brief meeting in his office. "I've not seen this before," Dennis said, his hands clasped tightly. "Usually, when our church hears about a new project, there's an energy in the room. Today, it felt more like … hesitation."

John and Dave nodded, and Dennis went on, "We've always been outwardly focused, and people have generously given their time and financial resources to help the church and community." Looking up as he was thinking about what to say next, he went on, "This project is an opportunity for us to have a kingdom impact on Clairemont and the surrounding area, one that might outlast each of us sitting here right now. I don't think we've ever had, or may ever get, such a wonderful opportunity." Christ's words came alive for Dennis, "The harvest is plentiful, but the workers are few" (Matthew 9:37).

Then Dennis asked, "Why do you think there's not more excitement and energy for the community center?"

John didn't hesitate. "Finances," he said, going straight to the heart of the issue. Then he recounted having overheard people say, "I know it's a good cause, but we just paid off the sanctuary remodel," and "I can't give any more right now. I wish they'd wait a year."

Dave chimed in, "Our people have gone above and beyond for a long time, Dennis. Between that and the economy, they're feeling financial strain, and they know this could be our biggest ask yet." He went on, "But it's not just about the money. People are tired. We've had a lot of asks in the last few years. Mission trips, the sanctuary renovation, the local food bank. It adds up."

Nodding in agreement, Dennis said, "I appreciate both of you and your honesty because too often issues like these don't make their way to me. Jesus always spoke the truth, and I want to know the truth about how people are feeling and what they're thinking. Sometimes I wonder if people are afraid to be honest with me because they incorrectly assume I'll think less of them. What else am I missing?"

Dave added, "We have another issue. It's come to my attention that Martha was hurt that she wasn't chosen to help lead the project. We all know she's a tireless worker on behalf of the church so she's feeling overlooked right now."

Dennis replied, "I'm thankful for Martha's contributions but I have to follow what I believe was the Lord's leading in choosing John."

John listened carefully, "I think that's why we need to approach this differently. What if, instead of asking for money, we asked people to give time and talent first?" He understood small steps in the right direction engaged consistency and could build momentum, making it easier for bigger commitments down the road.

Dennis and Dave both agreed that might be the right way to go. Then Dennis asked, "What should we do about Martha?"

John immediately volunteered, "Let me speak with Martha." The two were familiar with each other but had never had a conversation.

"I'll start reaching out to my contacts to see what else I can learn about how the congregation is feeling," Dave added.

Chapter 13 – Martha, Martha

"Thank you both," Dennis said. With that, the three stood up and the meeting ended.

***

For the next few days John pondered how and when to approach Martha. Little did he know, the opportunity would naturally present itself. It was Wednesday afternoon and John stopped by the church to meet with Dave. He and Martha almost bumped into each other as they rounded a corner coming from opposite directions.

"I'm sorry, Martha," he said as they adjusted themselves after the near mishap. "We've never been formally introduced. I'm John Andrews," he said, extending his hand.

Martha's expression was a mix of surprise and something else—caution, perhaps. Her posture remained stiff, as if she wanted to pivot and walk away. A little unsure of herself for a moment because of the abruptness of everything, Martha quickly righted herself and gave John a firm handshake, looking him directly in the eye. "Nice to *finally* meet you, John," she said with an emphasis on the word "finally" which didn't escape John's notice.

Martha remembered a time in her corporate career when she'd been passed over for a promotion. She'd worked twice as hard as her colleagues, but when the opportunity came, they chose someone else—someone who hadn't put in the same effort. That sting of being unappreciated still lingered. It felt like history was repeating itself.

John could sense an invisible wall between the two, so hoping to break down the barrier, he replied, "Martha, I should have approached you sooner. I apologize for not doing so. This is all new to me, so it's been kind of a whirlwind."

"I know it can be difficult because dealing with church matters is quite a bit different than business," Martha said in a tone that led John to believe she wanted him to know that she understood the church better than he did and felt she should have been the one to lead the community center project.

John rarely got offended, and understanding she felt slighted, he graciously replied, "Abigail has kept me up to date on church-related activities over the years, so I know you've been a part of the church for a long time and have helped with many projects."

Martha looked at him but didn't reply. She had mastered the art of guarding her thoughts—a habit shaped by years of needing to prove herself.

"It's been on my radar to reach out to you regarding the community center and now suddenly we bump into each other," he said with a smile, as if he knew it was a divine appointment.

Because of how Martha was feeling about everything, her focus wasn't on God at that moment. Divine timing never entered her mind—frustration had clouded her focus.

"Martha, this project will not be as successful as it could be without your participation," John said with sincerity. Martha faintly smiled and had a look on her face that conveyed, "You're darn right!"

"I thought you had it all figured out," she said with a hint of sarcasm.

John proceeded, "Hardly. Would you be open to meeting to explore how you could help?"

Despite how she felt about everything, she loved the church and had worked tirelessly for it since joining, so she agreed to meet John Thursday morning.

Before they knew it, the next day rolled around, and they were sitting in the church lobby. Never one to mince words, shortly after getting seated Martha told John, "I think we're moving too quickly on this project. People are feeling financial strain, and we might not come close to getting the funds we'll likely need."

Much to her surprise, John agreed. After a short pause, he said, "Is that a bad thing? If we can see how all of this will work out, then where does faith come in?"

She replied, "It's not always that simple. God wants us to be good stewards but I'm not sure we're doing that. I've seen churches go into debt over 'trusting God' before. We have other projects we need to keep going and we're struggling to get the volunteers we need. On top of

Chapter 13 – Martha, Martha

that, getting approval from the zoning board will be a bigger challenge than you might realize. Victoria has sway over more than just the city council and school board."

"Martha, you're worried about so many things but only one thing is important. Is God in this? If He is, nothing will stop it. He will be the one to soften hearts and remove the obstacles. We will simply be His tools in doing so. Do you believe God is in this?"

When John said she was worried about so many things, she suddenly felt convicted. Because of her name, she was intimately familiar with the story of Mary and Martha from the Bible—and at that moment, it felt painfully personal. Like the Martha who knew Jesus, she was a take charge person. She had to be during her career to earn respect in the male-dominated business world. And like Martha, she'd always provided the helping hands at church. Not by coincidence, she also knew she could get easily offended when others didn't appear to put in the kind of effort that she did.

Softening a bit she replied, "John, I'll be honest with you. I do believe God is in it and maybe that's all the more reason I was hurt when Dennis didn't even consider me. Or perhaps I should say, when God didn't put me on Dennis's heart to lead this. I've given so much to this church, John and sometimes I wonder if anyone even sees it—or if it matters."

John looked at her and replied, "I know God notices and cares, and so do I. That's why this conversation is taking place. Sometimes we receive what we long for—but not in the way we imagined. Think about all of the people in the Bible to whom God made promises but they often didn't materialize in the time or manner that they expected. But God was always faithful to His word."

"John, I'm not sure where I fit into this," Martha said. "But I do want to help. Maybe I could start by reviewing the project timeline—see if we can break it into manageable phases."

John's face lit up. "That would be perfect. Your experience could help us avoid so many pitfalls. This is exactly why I wanted to meet with you."

It was at that point that Martha and John began to turn a corner in their relationship. It would not only benefit them as friends, but it would also prove to be hugely beneficial for the church in time.

As John left the church, he felt a cautious optimism. Martha hadn't fully committed, but she'd taken a step in the right direction. John knew influence wasn't about a single moment—it was built over time, on trust, grace, and understanding. He whispered a prayer as he started his car, "Lord, keep softening Martha's heart. Help us build a strong partnership for the good of the church and the project."

> **Reflection:** Authentic influence often begins not in grand speeches, but in quiet moments of reconciliation. Like Martha, we can carry wounds from being overlooked or unappreciated—but God sees, and He invites us to serve in ways that may surprise us. John's gentle approach reminds us that hearts are softened not by pressure, but by presence. Where might God be calling you to lay down hurt and pick up purpose—trusting that His plans, even when unexpected, are always for your good?

Chapter 14 – An Inspired Idea

"But if any of you lacks wisdom, let him ask of God, who gives to all generously and without reproach, and it will be given to him."

—James 1:5

While John was smoothing things over with Martha, Dave was having conversations with various small group leaders in the church to gauge how the congregation felt about the community center. While most church leaders were excited, they told Dave many in their groups felt lukewarm about the community center. As he, Dennis, and John suspected, the hesitation stemmed from financial strain and volunteer fatigue. People felt stretched to the limit on both.

"People are worried, Dave," one small group leader said. "It's not just about money—it's about energy. Some of our folks are already volunteering several times a week."

Another leader added, "And there's a sense of weariness. We've been in project mode for years. Mission trips, the food pantry, the renovated sanctuary. It feels like we never get to rest."

Dave listened carefully. He knew the congregation wasn't lacking in faith—it was just exhausted. Then Dave got some unexpected news; two families would be leaving the church soon. Their departure had nothing to do with what was going on; rather, it was job relocation. Unfortunately, these were two families that were among the most generous givers.

Dave met with Dennis and John to fill them in on all that he'd learned. While it was disappointing, they still believed God was in it and would provide a way. They knew there would be challenges with the zoning board but were confident they'd come to some agreement after winning a solid majority of the city council. They decided to turn their attention to the congregation. Rather than call a separate meeting, Dennis decided to address the issue during Sunday's services, when attendance would be highest.

***

Sunday rolled around and Dennis opened saying, "No sermon this morning—what I need to share is just as important as any message I could preach. Many weeks ago, you heard me lay out a vision for a community center and last week I shared the good news that the city council approved the project. I believe with all my heart that the vision is from God and will have a huge impact on the people in our town, both young and old. It's our way to fulfill the Lord's calling, 'Truly I say to you, to the extent that you did it to one of these brothers of Mine, even the least of them, you did it to Me'" (Matthew 25:40).

He continued with a passionate plea, acknowledging how much he'd asked of people in the past and honestly telling them this would be difficult too. "I know this feels like a lot," Dennis said, "But God doesn't call us to what's easy—He calls us to what's needed. And right now, our community needs this." He concluded by reminding the congregation of several stories in the Bible were people felt overwhelmed, but God was always faithful. After concluding, he opened the floor for questions.

Silence settled over the room—heavy and uncertain. Dennis felt the weight of their unspoken concerns. This was not the breakthrough he had hoped for. It took a good while before anyone approached the mic to address Dennis and the congregation.

A man in his mid-30s with a young family was the first to speak. "Pastor, you know we love you, but I know I speak for many when I say, we're tapped out. I simply can't give any more, financially or physically. Prices on everything have gone up and I've not gotten a raise in several

Chapter 14 – An Inspired Idea

years. The math just doesn't add up. I feel like the Israelites—asked to make bricks without straw."

After that, another, then another member of the church echoed the same sentiments. Even the few people who encouraged everyone to trust God were overwhelmed by the number who felt unable to give any more than they were currently doing. A few said they would be reducing their giving in order to make ends meet.

John and Abigail sat silently and listened. Abigail wasn't just concerned about the project; she was equally concerned for John. He felt he'd found purpose, the kind with eternal consequences, but it looked like it might fall apart before their eyes.

For his part, John was disappointed but not discouraged. He reflected on all that had transpired so far that clearly showed God's hand in this; Joshua handing out Gideon Bibles, God showing him the connection between faith and influence, the council meeting, and his impromptu conversation with Martha, to name just a few. He remained confident and silently prayed, "Lord, show us what to do." Almost immediately an inspired idea came to mind. He wondered if it was God's answer to his prayer or just his own thoughts.

Abigail could see he was no longer paying attention to the noise in the room because he was in deep thought. After a few moments, she asked what he was thinking about. He briefly shared the idea and his self-doubt. Believing it was God, she encouraged him to take a step of faith. With the urgency of the moment, there was no time to run it by Dennis or Dave. Following Abigail's encouragement, he made the decision to trust the Lord and share it with the congregation. If he didn't, and they lost the support of the church, they might not get city approval again in the future, especially if Victoria had her way.

John asked for the mic and made his way to the front of the room. He stood below the stage—intentionally—wanting everyone to know he was one of them. He began, "Since retiring, and especially since I told Dennis I would take the lead on the community center, I've come to know many of you. Between that and all that Abigail has shared with me over the years, I have to say, I'm so impressed with your generosity of time, effort, and finances. But there are times when you feel tapped out—like you can't give one ounce or one dollar more. It's not just a feeling; you're at the end of your rope. Having said that, I believe God can enable us to do more than we think possible and to do that, He provides. As I listened to the conversation I prayed. 'Lord, show us what to do,' and I believe He showed me."

The room was quiet at John's bold proclamation. He surveyed the congregation then continued, "This is a community center, so why not involve the community? What if people in the community were allowed to contribute and work side-by-side with us? And not just individuals but businesses too. After all, many local businesses support our sports boosters and other activities around town. Perhaps we can influence them to participate with us. We'll retain leadership over the center, but they'll be co-creators with us—giving time, talent, and resources."

With another pause, he could see people nodding and whispering to one another. Eventually a hand went up, so John walked over to the lady and gave her the mic.

"I like the idea," she said, then went on, "I was at the council meeting. I know one council member thought the community center was just a cover for evangelizing to unsuspecting kids. I think participation from individuals and organizations outside of the church would help alleviate any concerns around that."

"Why would anyone outside our church want to help us with this?" asked one person.

"What if businesses try to take over?" another man asked. "I don't want this turning into a commercial venture."

"That's a valid concern," John said. "We'll set clear guidelines. Our goal is community partnership, not corporate sponsorship."

Immediately someone else chimed in, "Many of us might already be their customers and it could end up being good for their businesses."

Another member added, "In addition to giving us some relief, business owners who participate might see the growing character of the young people. That could lead them to offer some of the kids part time work when they're old enough." Many heads nodded upon hearing that.

Chapter 14 – An Inspired Idea

"I run a small plumbing business," a man said. "I'd be willing to donate some labor if it helps. I might not have extra money, but I can give time."

Suddenly, the tide was turning—momentum building with each voice. As people made more and more positive comments, it created a snowball effect until a solid majority was on board. The church may not be able to get more resources internally, but they had the backing of the congregation to try bringing in community partners.

Dennis approached John after the service and thanked him. "John, I would never have come up with that solution to our problem in a million years."

"Believe me, Dennis—it never would've come to me if I hadn't prayed and taken that step of faith," John said. "Besides, aren't you the one who told me God is always speaking to us and that we have to open our hearts and listen with our eyes and ears?"

Dennis smiled and said, "John, you're a fast learner and a very good listener."

While there was much to celebrate for gaining consensus with the congregation, what no one realized was that Victoria was doing her best to manipulate the zoning board.

Days later she learned about the congregation meeting and John's idea to bring the community into the project. If John thought this would make her back down, he was mistaken. She pulled out her phone and began typing a message to a business owner she knew. "Hey, just heard the church wants to involve local businesses in their project. Before you commit, you might want to know what they're really about. Let's talk." She hit send, knowing that a few well-placed doubts could unravel even the best-laid plans. Doubt was already taking root—Victoria was making sure of it.

> **Reflection:** When God gives a vision, He also provides the wisdom to see it through—but sometimes, His provision comes in unexpected ways. John's inspired idea was born not from strategy,

but from surrender. In moments of discouragement, do you stop to ask, "Lord, show me what to do"? Faith isn't about having all the answers—it's about trusting the One who does and stepping forward when He calls.

Chapter 15 – The Opposition's Next Move

"He (Sanballat) spoke in the presence of his brothers and the wealthy men of Samaria and said, 'What are these feeble Jews doing? Are they going to restore it [the wall] for themselves?'"

—Nehemiah 4:2

After gaining the congregation's support for involving the broader community, Dennis, John, and Dave turned their attention to local businesses and the zoning board. Dennis and Dave took the lead with the town's businesses. Dennis had strong standing in the community, thanks to years of outreach led by The Rock. Dave, having owned a small business in town and his involvement with several business associations, was a natural to help spearhead the effort. It was determined that John would reach out to businesses outside town as well as focusing on dealing with the zoning board. Meanwhile, John decided to reach out to Victoria, hoping to soften her stance.

As John might have guessed, Victoria was already working hard to put up roadblocks because she was still incensed at how the city council meeting had ended. She began working the zoning board, applying the same tactics she'd used on the city council. From experience she knew that just because the city council approved a project, that didn't necessarily mean it was a done deal. The zoning board could reject a project for a variety of reasons, and if that happened, at a minimum the community center would be delayed or may never get going. She started with Tim Rhodes.

Like Victoria, Tim had lived in Clairemont most of his life, so the two had known each other since grade school. During their childhood, the textile industry was the main employer in town. Most of those jobs left in the 1990s, so the town had to reinvent itself. It was able to do so by adding local shops, restaurants, and investing in its infrastructure. That revitalization helped Clairemont to become a desirable home for those working in nearby Charlotte.

Tim grew up going to church with his parents, as most kids did in town during those years, but he was not a religious man. That was evidenced by the fact that he'd not attended church since college. However, unlike Victoria, he wasn't adamantly opposed to faith-based initiatives.

"Tim, I know you're a lot like me," Victoria opened the conversation. "I have no issues with religion, as long as it's kept to church and personal beliefs. The city council approved The Rock's request to build a community center, but I still believe it's not a good idea."

When Victoria paused Tim interjected, "I know about the project. We're supposed to meet with representatives from the church soon. A community center seems like a good thing for the town, so I don't understand why you're so opposed to it." He'd heard about the fallout from the council meeting from more than one person.

Victoria reiterated her beliefs about separation of church and state, concerns over proselytizing, and a few other issues she had with the project. By now she'd shared her views on the community center so often that she was able to clearly articulate her position as if she was making a presentation.

Tim pressed, "You know the whole separation of church and state argument doesn't apply here. If it was as you say, we'd never let any church put up a building in town." After sharing his views regarding her other concerns, he got to the heart of the matter when he asked, "Victoria, what's your real reason for opposing the project?"

She tried to reiterate her stance by going back to her talking points, but Tim wasn't buying it. He asked again, "I hear what you're saying but it doesn't make sense to me. When I went to college and stopped going to church, I realized I didn't miss it, that it was important for my parents

Chapter 15 – The Opposition's Next Move

but not me. I remember you enjoyed church when we were young but there came a time when I never saw you there again. Did something happen that's affecting your stance on the community center?"

Victoria was a private person, so she wasn't about to talk about her family and her father leaving. Truth be told, even she hadn't fully connected the dots on the impact of his abandonment and her feelings about religion. If she were honest with Tim, she would have said she thought churches were filled with a bunch of hypocrites. However, a statement like that could offend more people than it would win to her way of thinking, and she didn't want to jeopardize her positions on the council and school board. She simply told Tim, "Personal feelings have no place in decisions like this. I take a rational approach, so my vote is always based on what's best for the town."

Tim laughed because he knew there was no way to separate personal feelings from professional decisions fully. He knew Victoria well enough to let it go because she wasn't going to reveal her true motive or feelings. As she was getting up to leave, he said, "If the church community center meets our building codes, I'll give it the green light and will encourage the other board members to do the same."

Victoria forced a smile. "Good to see you, Tim. You do what you think is right—I'll do the same." Tim had a strong sense this wasn't over as far as Victoria was concerned.

As she drove home, she thought about Tim mentioning her enjoying church when she was young. In a moment of honesty, she admitted to herself that he was right. She loved church and the youth activities as a child. But that all changed when her father packed up and left without so much as a goodbye.

Her mind wandered back to the day he had left. She was 12, sitting on the front porch, waiting for him to come home. He never did. The only thing he left behind was his Bible, still open on the kitchen table. Even now, the sight of a Bible stirred something sharp inside her—anger, abandonment, pain.

Often, the wounds inflicted by earthly fathers distort how we view our heavenly Father. Victoria had carried that burden for decades, unaware.

When our fathers do things that hurt us, it's not uncommon to project that behavior on to God. That's where Victoria had been for decades even though she didn't realize it because she'd stuffed her feelings so deep within her that she rarely felt anything but anger when it came to church. As she continued to drive, she felt a tear stream down her face. Rather than yield to what she was feeling, like a child who was being punished, she stiffened her upper lip and resolve, unwilling to yield to the truth.

Victoria had meetings with several other zoning board members, and most were of the same opinion that Tim held; as long as the building plans met city guidelines, the center would be approved. Despite that, Victoria was still hopeful that the seeds of doubt she was planning might cause delays or other hardships.

***

Since catching wind of the church's idea to include private funds from local businesses, she'd continued to text people. Her resolve only strengthened when she didn't have the success she'd hoped for with the zoning board. She devised another plan of attack. Her next move: approach the town's prominent business owners—quietly sowing doubt, one conversation at a time. Her pitch was always the same with each person. Not wanting to seem hostile, she would start by acknowledging a community center would be good for Clairemont and that it was a generous offer from The Rock to build it.

Next, she would start sowing seeds of doubt. She steered clear of the separation of church and state argument because of the resistance she'd seen from some people to that line of thinking. Truthfully, even she knew it was flimsy at best. Instead, she zeroed in on the religious aspect of the community center.

Her first stop was Samuel Levitt—a well-respected business owner whose furniture store had served Clairemont since the 1950s. It was one of the last remaining Jewish-owned businesses in town.

Victoria knew Sam's family history and asked, "Sam, given your Jewish faith, would you want your kids going to an overtly Christian

Chapter 15 – The Opposition's Next Move

community center?" She was being manipulative because she knew John told the city council there would be no Christian teaching, only that universal principles like loving your neighbor, respect for all people, being generous givers, and a few others would be foundational.

She could see he was thinking hard about her statement. He said, "I suppose if I found out my kids were being exposed to an overtly religious message, I would not allow them to go."

Victoria seized the opening. "Sam, that would put you in a bind. If your kids were enjoying the community center, suddenly you'd be the bad guy for not allowing them to go. That would be the case for other parents who might not want their kids in that atmosphere. Having been part of the school board for a long time, I've seen the negative impact on kids when they feel excluded."

Sam nodded in agreement, so she made her final move to win him to her way of thinking. "I know the project will have a price tag that's more than the church can afford. I've heard they will be soliciting local businesses for donations to make up the difference." She went on, "Because of my role on the city council, I'm in constant contact with business owners in town. Very few are interested in participating in the project because of the kinds of issues we've just discussed." That was a lie—but one she delivered smoothly, knowing it would trigger doubt. She'd not talked with many business owners about the project yet. However, she knew if she let him, or any other business owner, know most were against the business funding aspect, it would be easier for that person to follow suit. It was classic manipulation—leveraging false social proof to push him toward fear.

Part of Sam wanted to dismiss Victoria's concerns, but something about the way she phrased everything nagged at him. Could this project alienate families who didn't share Christian beliefs? Would his support cost him customers? He shifted in his seat. His grandfather had built this business on integrity and relationships. He didn't want to jeopardize that. Could his involvement in the community center send the wrong message? He hated that the thought even crossed his mind—but now the seed was planted.

Victoria knew Sam, despite his friendship with John and good relationship with many church members at The Rock, was now wavering regarding the project. He was someone John was counting on as much for his influence in the community as he was his financial support.

Her conversations always ended with, "I know someone from the church will eventually reach out to you. Again, I think the community center is a nice idea and whether or not you participate is entirely up to you. But I have to say, I think businesses that participate could alienate customers who don't hold the same views on religion." That last statement was meant to invoke scarcity, the fear of losing customers.

She didn't know how much the church would need to complete the project nor how many businesses might contribute but she was feeling very good about business owners thinking twice about their participation. Many saw through her strategy—but Victoria held influence in town, and no one wanted to be on her bad side.

Reflection: Opposition often strikes hardest when God's work gains momentum—but not all opposition is loud. Like Victoria, it may come through subtle doubts, whispered fears, or well-placed pressure. It's the same tactic Satan used with Eve in the garden, "Did God really say…?" John's story reminds us that influence used to serve is powerful—but influence used to control is dangerous. When faced with resistance, will you fall prey to fear—or step forward in truth, knowing God's plans cannot be undone by human schemes?

Chapter 16 – A Gentle Answer

"A gentle answer turns away wrath, but a harsh word stirs up anger."

—Proverbs 15:1

Though they had never met formally, John and Victoria were familiar with one another. John knew Victoria because of her active role in town politics and the school system. He knew her as someone who got things done—he'd even voted for her once. However, until now he had no idea about the tactics she used to secure her victories.

For her part, Victoria knew about John primarily because of his notoriety running MediTech. The company grew significantly under John's leadership and employed a good number of people in town. That meant that John enjoyed a good reputation with everyone in the area, including Victoria. That is, until the community center project was announced.

John had been praying about Victoria since the project was given the green light. Between his lengthy business career and leading MediTech for more than a decade, he knew her type well. He understood how much havoc one determined person could create—if she had influence, skill, and motivation. As he tried to decide on his best approach with Victoria, his mind wandered back to when he tried to get to know Braedon Stanton, an accountant at MediTech.

Braedon had been one of the toughest people for John to reach. None of John's usual approaches to influence worked with Braedon until he got to know him and understood what was going on in Braedon's life.

It wasn't that Braedon was a bad person or even standoffish by nature. His daughter's illness at a young age weighed heavily on him and that was the cause of his cold outward demeanor. Underneath that gruff exterior, Braedon was a wonderful person and the two had stayed in regular touch since John left MediTech.

John thought perhaps Victoria was similar, a good person under the conniving exterior, someone who had a story that might explain why she acted the way she did. He was sure of this; God loved Victoria as much as He loved John, Abigail, or anyone else. Then it struck him—perhaps God was using this turmoil to work something in Victoria's life. Rather than trying to control the situation, John trusted God to bring about a meeting in His own time. It was a risky move because with each passing day, that was more time for Victoria to sow tares with the zoning board and business owners.

***

John happened to run into Victoria five days later. He was downtown for lunch with a potential corporate partner then headed to the municipal building to start filing paperwork with the zoning board. As he walked through town towards the municipal building, he realized just how interconnected everything was. People didn't just live here—they knew one another's kids, coached Little League together, and ran into each other at the grocery store.

Before long, he arrived at the municipal building that had been built in the early 1940s. Back then, Clairemont was still a sleepy railroad town. Even after several renovations, the building still smelled faintly of old wood and ink—remnants of a time when everything was typed on manual typewriters and stored in metal filing cabinets.

Upon entering, he noticed Victoria talking with another council member. He walked up and said hello to both. Victoria's expression betrayed her—caught off guard, and clearly displeased by the unexpected encounter. She liked to be in control—and this was anything but. Nonetheless, she shook John's hand and said hello. The other council

Chapter 16 – A Gentle Answer

member, someone who had voted for the community center project, sensed something was up. He politely excused himself, leaving John and Victoria alone.

John started, "Victoria, sorry if I caught you off guard. I'm here to drop off some paperwork for the zoning board. When I saw you, I thought it might be more than coincidence. I'm sure you're busy, so I won't take up your time. Is your schedule open tomorrow, maybe 30 minutes, to sit down and talk?"

Without looking at her phone she said, "Unfortunately, I'm booked all day, John."

Early in his career John learned, after someone said no, if you're willing to concede a little, quite often they'll make a concession in return. It was a natural use of reciprocity. He said, "I thought my chances were slim on a day's notice. How does your schedule look the day after?"

Victoria pulled out her phone and glanced at her calendar. "I'm sorry John, the next few days aren't good either." The truth was, she had openings but didn't want to meet with him on such short notice because she wanted time to ready herself for the encounter.

Undeterred he casually replied, "I get it. The community center is keeping me busier than I anticipated. However, I have a good bit of flexibility. Since you have your phone out, could you let me know when you have an opening next? I'd be happy to rearrange my schedule to meet with you."

Feeling cornered, and unwilling to lie again, she blurted, "I'm open next Monday at 8:30 a.m."

Because this was so important, without looking at his phone he said, "I can do that. Should I meet you here at your office or somewhere else?" He knew meeting in her office would allow her to feel more comfortable. Not wanting to give up home field advantage, she forced a smile and said, "My office is fine."

John thanked her for her flexibility, and they parted ways. John headed down one hallway to drop off the paperwork and Victoria quickly moved in the opposite direction towards her office. She was not pleased with what had just transpired and thought about canceling the meeting. She wasn't sure why she agreed to meet with John. Maybe it was curiosity, or maybe—though she'd never admit it—she was tired of fighting. Knowing John's persistence, she reasoned she'd eventually have to meet him sometime so she might as well get it over with.

John happened to see Tim when he was dropping off the zoning board information. After a brief, cordial exchange he said, "Tim, I know you and Victoria grew up here. I'm guessing you both love the community and that's why you've stayed. We both know she's opposed to the community center. Even though we got approval, I'd sure feel better if she saw the potential good for the town and was not so adamantly opposed. Without breaking any confidences that might exist between the two of you, is there anything you can share that might help me understand her better?"

Tim liked John and was happy to share his insights. Everything he shared was public knowledge, but some information was new to John. He let John know she really had a passion for the kids and that's why she got on the school board so long ago. Next, he said something that caught John's attention, "Given how much she cares about kids, I've always been surprised she never had any of her own." John tucked that away in the back of his mind.

After John asked a few casual questions, Tim proceeded to tell John about Victoria approaching him regarding the zoning. "John, I'm not a religious man but I think what Dennis has done with The Rock has been great for our town. Most cities across this state would welcome any organization that does the good things all of you have done for us. It almost makes me reconsider my stance on religion," he said with a grin.

John replied with a smile, "Nothing is impossible, Tim."

Tim concluded telling John about Victoria having been very involved in church when she was young but that all changed when her dad suddenly left the family. Beyond that, he couldn't understand why she was so dug in on this issue.

In the ensuing days, John did all he could to learn about Victoria and her background, but nothing was as valuable as what Tim shared. John had a strong feeling that she harbored resentment against the church because of her father, which might explain her stance against

Chapter 16 – A Gentle Answer

the project and why she never married. He ran his thoughts by Abigail knowing whatever he shared would go no further. She concurred with John and let him know she'd be praying for Victoria, not just to come around on the community center but for her inner peace.

Monday morning rolled around, and John's focus had shifted—from convincing Victoria to simply getting to know her. Whether or not she came on board, he knew her own peace was more important because he knew that it was for God. The irony was, if she found that peace, he had no doubt she would become a supporter because when a person's heart changes, everything changes.

John arrived at her office five minutes early and took a seat. The admin for the city council members let Victoria know he was there. At 8:37, Victoria finally came out to meet John. No one emerged from her office, and he knew she wasn't on a call because he could hear the conversation between her and the admin. Classic power play—but John let it go. He was happy to have the opportunity finally to have a real conversation with her.

In a businesslike, matter of fact tone, Victoria said, "Sorry for the delay John. How can I help you?" It was a typical opening for a politician who thought everyone wants something.

"Victoria, to put you at ease, I assure you that I'm not here to convince you on anything regarding the community center. Whether or not we see things the same and whether or not we work together going forward, I just want to get to know you as a person."

Victoria was skeptical. Her view of people differed from John's. Perhaps it was her past or a bit of cynicism from her time in politics, but she thought everyone was out for themself. Sadly, that attitude even extended to her friends. She saw offers to help as "give and take," never just an act of kindness. She was blunt, "John, I've been in politics a long time. Everyone wants something so let's cut to the chase. I'm not shifting my stance on the community center for all the reasons I shared during the council meeting."

Unfazed, John said, "That's alright, Victoria. I respect your stance. Most people don't have strong convictions, and I know it takes a lot to hold on to them, especially when others may not agree. We don't know each other but I hope you'll take me at my word, I'm simply here to get to know you better. Once this project is done, we'll still both be residents of this town, and I'd like for us to be able to get along and perhaps one day even call each other friend."

Victoria could hear the sincerity in his tone, and she could see it in his eyes, it wasn't a look that she was familiar with, but she knew it was true. She softened a bit and said, "While that sounds nice John, I've never seen a situation where people who disagreed on something as important as this struck up a friendship."

John smiled. "You know history, Victoria. President Reagan and Speaker Tip O'Neill had a very contentious relationship when it came to their views on how best to run the government. But according to everyone who knew both men, when 5:00 p.m. rolled around and work was over the two were friends and even shared drinks together. I know we live in a different world today, but I still believe that kind of relationship is possible."

He could see Victoria was considering what he had just said but before she could say anything he went on, "I know you have a heart for children. I suspect that's why you ran for the school board even though you had no kids in the school system. I have a heart for children too. Mine are grown up and out of the house but I remember those days when they were in school and how important after-school activities were. I'm not saying this to try to convince you of the community project. I'm only telling this to you because I think we have this in common; what's best for the kids in our community. I'm sure if we got to know each other we'd realize we had lots more in common as well. Two heads are better than one. Even if we don't agree on everything, together we might find better solutions than we could alone. That would benefit the community."

Victoria found herself agreeing with John but couldn't bring herself to admit it. She wasn't one to let her guard down and her views on human nature were not about to change that quickly. However, the conversation became less contentious and more informal. Before she realized it, the conversation felt less like politics—and more like friendship.

Chapter 16 – A Gentle Answer

John could sense the transformation but didn't want to push it. He glanced at his watch and said, "I know we only set aside 30 minutes and it's five till nine right now. I want to be respectful of your time. I really did enjoy getting to know you a little better so I'd like to ask, would you be open to another conversation?"

Victoria wasn't sure what was happening. She had expected another fight, another battle of wills, but something about John's approach made it difficult to maintain her guard. Always looking for an ally and thinking she might need John's help in the future, she replied, "I'd be willing to do that under one condition. We refrain from talking about the community center again. Is that fair?"

"Fair enough," he said.

Before he left, they looked at their calendars and found another time the following week to continue the conversation in her office. John had not set a specific goal for that first meeting but he left feeling he'd made tremendous progress.

Reflection: Influence doesn't always require actively trying to persuade—sometimes it begins with simply listening. John's gentle approach disarmed resistance, not by force, but by seeking connection instead of control. When we shift our focus from winning to understanding, hearts can begin to soften. Who in your life needs less argument—and more grace? A listening ear and gentle answer, spoken with sincerity, might open the door to healing you never expected.

Chapter 17 – Winning Hearts, Not Just Minds

"I will give you a new heart and put a new spirit within you; and I will remove the heart of stone from your flesh and give you a heart of flesh."

—*Ezekiel 36:26*

When Victoria agreed to another meeting, even she was surprised. There was something different about John—he wasn't pushing an agenda. He was just present, and she appreciated it. She found herself drawn to John's genuine desire to know her—not persuade her. Unlike so many others, he wasn't angling for anything. She truly believed that even if her stance on the community center never changed, he would be just as interested in maintaining a friendship. John was living out the principle of liking—not to gain an advantage, but to love as Christ would. The more he got to know Victoria, the more he cared about her well-being and hoped that one day she might make her way back to the faith she had as a child.

Before leaving her office that day he said, "Victoria, I enjoyed our conversation. If there's anything I can help you with, don't hesitate to reach out." She almost couldn't believe her ears. She knew John was sincere in his offer to help and there were no strings attached. As he walked out, she struggled to make sense of why he would have any desire to help her after all she'd done to sabotage the community center.

***

Chapter 17 – Winning Hearts, Not Just Minds

Despite their budding relationship, the seeds Victoria had planted among local business owners had begun to take root. That was evident because Dennis and Dave were running into more roadblocks than open roads. Aware of John's meetings with Victoria, Dennis and Dave asked for a sit-down.

The three met in the sanctuary at the church. Dennis asked John, "How are things going with the zoning board?" John told him the paperwork was filed and soon a meeting would be set to discuss the plans and cover any issues the board might have.

Dennis went on, "That's good news. But I've heard Victoria's been talking to zoning board members. Should we be concerned?"

"I don't think so. Unlike the city council, we don't have to win anyone over. It's more about making sure we cross all the Ts and dot all the Is as far as their requirements go. I'm aware that Victoria spoke to a few people. In fact, Tim Rhodes told me about their conversation. Although he isn't a churchgoer, it sounded like he had more issues with Victoria's position than he did with our plans."

Dave chimed in, "I know you've had a few meetings with Victoria. Any luck winning her over?"

"Not exactly," John opened. He could see a look of disappointment on Dennis and Dave's faces. "When I met with Victoria, I promised not to bring up the community center."

"Why would you do that?" Dennis asked with an exasperated tone.

"Dennis, think about your approach to people outside the faith. You always say, 'Come as you are.' That's how I'm approaching Victoria—no pressure, just presence."

"With all due respect, John," Dave said, "We don't have time for a therapy session. We need her to stop blocking us."

"I get that," John replied. "But influence isn't just about winning minds—it's about reaching hearts. I believe if we show Victoria real kindness, the kind we preach, the rest will follow."

Dennis sighed, rubbing his chin. "You know, John, I preach patience and yet I wasn't practicing it just now. I guess I'm just so focused on gaining zoning board approval that I forgot this is about more than a building. Shame on me for putting the cart before the horse. I'm like anyone else and can lose sight of the big picture. Lately, I've been more focused on getting approval than caring for the people involved. That's not who I want to be."

Feeling a similar conviction, and a little embarrassed at his last statement, Dave nodded in agreement.

"If Victoria's heart changes, I'm sure she'll become a supporter but that's a byproduct. The more I've learned about her, the more I want to see her come back to the faith that meant so much to her when she was young. I have a sense there's a lot of hurt and distrust behind her opposition. Whether or not she becomes an advocate, I think we're gaining the support we need," John confidently said.

Dave began to let John know they might not have as much support as he thought. "John, we're running into more roadblocks than we anticipated. We knew not everyone would want to participate but we've been surprised by the resistance. Unfortunately, Victoria is skilled—and many prominent people are hesitant because of her."

John let them know he was having success with businesspeople outside the town in the surrounding communities. That's probably because Victoria didn't have connections with those folks. Still, it would be more important to win over as many as possible within the town lest people outside wonder why there's not more support from the local community.

"Who is resistant that, if we win them over, might lead others to follow suit?" John asked.

Dave and Dennis replied at the same time, "Samuel Levitt."

"I know Sam quite well," John shared. "I'm surprised because he's been so generous with the town over the years."

Dennis and Dave proceeded to fill John in on the conversation with Sam. They let John know the resistance from others was along the same lines as Sam shared. That's why they clearly knew Victoria had made their way to each one before they did.

"Let me reach out to Sam. If we can win him back, others may follow," John proposed.

Chapter 17 – Winning Hearts, Not Just Minds

John knew influence was about wooing, winning others over, but it had to be done ethically. The principles of influence were neutral tools that could be used for good or evil. Knowing some of the animosity that existed between the Jewish and Christian communities over the centuries, he had to make sure there was no hint of manipulation when he talked with Sam.

For the most part, Sam enjoyed living in Clairemont and the townsfolk. While he'd not experienced much antisemitism from the locals, any time he did, it stung and lingered. He reasoned, no matter where he went, it was likely that he would experience the same. It was a sad reality that John was sensitive to because he'd seen it a few times over his career.

***

John met with Sam at Sam's office. After catching up on how their families were doing, they got down to business. John opened, "Sam, you know I'm here to talk about the community center. I know you met with Dennis and Dave and expressed your reservations about participating in the project. You and I have known each other a long time so I thought it would be good for me to address your concerns."

Sam countered, "John, I appreciate that you're taking time to meet with me. That says a lot about you and our friendship, and I respect that. However, I'm not sure you'll be able to alleviate my concerns if Dennis and Dave couldn't. Some say the community center is just a cover for evangelizing. I'm not opposed to faith, but I don't want to alienate my customers."

John was undeterred. He knew that the same message could land differently depending on who delivered it. It came down to liking and authority. It's always easier to say yes to those we know, like, and trust. Sam didn't have that to the same degree with Dennis and Dave, but John had established all three long ago with Sam, when nothing was on the line.

"I appreciate your friendship too, Sam. As a friend, you're free to say no and it won't change a thing between us. I don't think I'd be a good friend if I didn't give it a shot because I believe this project will be life changing for many people. Kids and parents will certainly benefit but I believe the volunteers will and so will those who support the center in other ways."

Sam was smiling because he always enjoyed talking with John and could see his sincerity. This wasn't about Sam's money—it was about offering him a chance to help change lives.

John went on, "Our town isn't necessarily divided but we could be a closer knit community. The center will bring people together in a whole different way, without focusing on politics, sports, religion, or anything else that so often separates people. It will be about helping kids. I assured the council, and give you my word, that there will be no overtly religious teaching. I purposely said 'overt' but want to be up front—there will be spiritual principles that guide us. However, I think they are ones that both of our faiths agree on; loving our neighbors as ourselves, extending respect to everyone, and being generous givers when it comes to our time and talents. Wouldn't you agree—those are values worth sowing into the next generation?" John always tried to phrase things in a question to allow whomever he was speaking with the opportunity to answer the question for themselves.

Sam couldn't disagree because he knew the overlap that existed between his Jewish faith and Christian tenets.

As John continued to share, he addressed all of the concerns Victoria had brought up but did so without naming her. John had no intention of turning Sam—or anyone else—against Victoria. Influence wasn't about division, but unity. Sam did bring up her name and, while John was concerned with the inroads she'd made, he graciously replied, "I'm starting to get to know Victoria. I respect that she has strong views and holds tightly to them. I wish more people had convictions like that. She's similar to us in that she wants what's best for our kids and the community. We just have differing views on how best to make that happen."

Sam exhaled, tapping his fingers against his desk, his thoughts swirling. He respected Victoria—she'd always been a straight shooter.

But more importantly, he trusted John. The two voices clashed in his mind, one urging caution, the other whispering possibility. But the longer Sam listened, the more he realized John was right. The logic was there. Even more than that, he could feel it. This was bigger than a business deal—it was about something deeper and by the end of the conversation he was on board. He jokingly said, "John, I never felt like I was being sold but, in the end, you sold me. How can I help make the community center a reality?"

John was overjoyed. It wasn't that he got what he wanted, it was that a friend would come alongside him and The Rock on such an important endeavor. They talked about finances, volunteering, and other ways to support the project.

John ended with, "Sam, one of the biggest things you can do is to help sway others who might have felt the way you did. I don't know all of those people the same way that I know you so I can't necessarily have the same conversation with them. Because you've known many for a long time, and they trust you, just knowing you're on board will carry a lot of weight. Would you be willing to be a vocal advocate?"

Sam pledged both his resources and reputation to the project.

As John left Sam's office, he felt a sense of momentum again. Sam's support was a turning point. But he knew Victoria wouldn't back down easily. Influence was a two-way street, and the next move might not be his to make.

> **Reflection:** Winning minds may bring agreement—but winning hearts brings transformation. John's journey reminds us that influence grounded in love changes lives. When we focus less on outcomes and more on genuine connection, we open space for God to move in unexpected ways. Who in your life needs less convincing—and more compassion? Remember, God often softens hearts through those willing to serve.

Chapter 18 – From the Mountain Top to the Wilderness

"The voice of one crying in the wilderness, 'Make ready the way of the Lord, Make His paths straight.'"

—Mark 1:3

Everything was progressing just as Dennis, John, and Dave had hoped for. While there had been long days and bumps along the way, they'd been able to deal with them effectively. Each day, the vision of the community center sharpened—no longer just a dream, but something real.

The zoning board reviewed all of the paperwork and asked John to come in to discuss some revisions to the plans. He excitedly shared the good news with Abigail. As he got ready for the meeting she asked, "How's Dave doing?"

"Fine. Why?" John replied.

"Beth is concerned. She said he's been putting in more hours than normal at the church and doesn't seem quite like himself," Abigail responded.

John, focused on the zoning board, dismissed it as the strain of hard work. He kissed her and made his way out the door.

At the municipal building he met Joe Walls, the architect of the project for The Rock. He asked Joe to join him to answer any detailed questions that might come up.

Joe had moved to Clairemont a few years earlier. About a decade before the move, he'd gone through a spiritual reawakening and got

Chapter 18 – From the Mountain Top to the Wilderness

involved in his local church in his prior town. As soon as he heard Dennis talk about his vision for the community center, he volunteered his expertise to draft plans for the building.

The zoning board meeting started well but then hit a sticking point regarding some aspects of the building. Understandably, Joe pushed back. After all, this project was special to him, it was like his baby, and he didn't want anyone messing with it. Based on his experience, he knew the plans were solid and felt they didn't need any revisions. The board thought differently.

The atmosphere began to get tense, and it seemed as if they were at an impasse. Sensing tension rising, John interjected, "Let's take a 15-minute break. Cooler heads usually find better solutions." Everyone thought that was a good idea, so they took a break.

John pulled Joe aside to discuss some of the issues that were raised by the board. "Joe, can I offer some advice?"

Nodding his head, but clearly frustrated, Joe said, "Sure."

John proceeded, "Rarely do we get *everything* we want in business or life. We need to be willing to compromise. If you hold fast to your position and the project is rejected, what might you look back on and wish you'd been willing to meet the board part way on?"

The thought of the project being dismissed outright because of his refusal to compromise caught Joe's attention. He was feeling the weight of scarcity and did not want to be the reason the community center didn't come into existence.

Joe exhaled; eyes fixed on the blueprint. His masterpiece was now a battlefield for differing ideas. He hated making changes, but he hated the idea of losing the project even more. He nodded. "Alright, John. Let's get this done."

They continued talking and Joe shared a few things he would be willing to compromise on. John gave him a little coaching, discussed their strategy, and they returned to the room where everyone was already seated.

John opened, invoking the principle of unity, "While we'd love to see our plans green lighted as is, we know that's not going to happen.

But here's the thing we need to keep front and center—we all want the same thing, a safe place where our kids and others in the community can come together."

Everyone nodded in agreement. Stan spoke for the board, "Thank you, John. We've never drawn a line in the sand we weren't willing to reconsider. How do you propose we proceed?"

At that, John and Joe shared an area of compromise, knowing if they did so first, reciprocity would dictate a move to the middle from the board. Then, invoking reciprocity again, they asked for a concession in return. The conversation became more amicable as the two sides negotiated their way to an agreement. After an hour they finalized the agreement. The community center would break ground in 30 days!

As John and Joe walked out together, Joe thanked John. "John, when an architect creates plans for a building, we do so believing it's perfect as is. I can get very defensive when someone questions my work or makes suggestions. It frustrates me that they can't see things my way or question my expertise."

"I get it, Joe. It's not unlike whenever I had a vision for MediTech. I used to want standing ovations for my brilliance," he said with a laugh. "But I've learned vision needs give and take. I had to learn the art of give and take to make the vision a reality. Truthfully, after some back and forth, what we came up with was almost always better than what I initially proposed. I believe the center will be stronger because of today's compromise."

Joe agreed and John went on, "I know you don't consider yourself a salesperson but when you're trying to win approval on a project, you're selling yourself and your idea. Knowing that, you'd do well to learn a little about influence. A resource that helped me was Robert Cialdini's book, *Influence: The Psychology of Persuasion*."

Joe said he'd pick up the book and John told him he'd be happy to talk with him about how to put the concepts into practice.

***

Chapter 18 – From the Mountain Top to the Wilderness

It was about 4 p.m. when John called Dennis to see if he and Dave were at the church. Dennis let John know they were both there for another hour or so. John said he'd swing by to talk with them in person about the zoning board meeting. He gave no hint that they'd gotten final approval because he wanted to share the good news in person so they could celebrate together. It had only been a few months since they started working together but it felt like much longer because of the trials they'd encountered and all that they had accomplished.

The three met in Dennis's office. Trying to contain the good news, John opened with a sigh, "Joe and I met with the zoning board this afternoon and they had a lot of changes they'd like to see." He let out another sigh, as if exasperated, then went on, "It got so contentious we had to stop the meeting."

Dennis and Dave anticipated John would talk about delays but instead he said, "However, after a short break to cool the temperature in the room, and a little coaching with Joe, we got the deal done!"

"Holy cow!" Dennis exclaimed. "This is beyond great! I can't thank you two enough for your leadership." Dennis glanced at the calendar on his desk and started laughing.

Dave asked, "What's so funny?"

"Do you realize it was 52 days ago when the three of us first met to officially kick off this project?" Dennis asked. "Nehemiah rebuilt Jerusalem's walls in 52 days—and it took us 52 days to get permission to start building our walls. That's no coincidence!"

Their celebration would be short lived.

Dave told the two he had a few things to get done so he excused himself. John noticed Dave glancing at his watch—distracted, distant, not his usual steady self. It concerned John so he said to Dennis, "Dave's always been steady, the kind of man who kept his word and his schedule. But have you noticed that lately, he's been harder to pin down, sometimes showing up a little late or staying behind when everyone has else left?"

"You must be more perceptive than me, John. We're all busy and have lots to do," Dennis replied.

Given what Abigail shared about Beth's concerns, John made a mental note to check in with Dave next time they were together.

By now it was well past 5 p.m. so Dennis decided to head home to share the good news with his wife. John said he'd walk out with him.

As John and Dennis made their way down the hall, a pretty young woman passed them. Dennis was looking down, talking the whole time so he didn't notice her. She caught John's attention because he'd never seen her at the church before and she was dressed up as if she were going out on the town. As quickly as she caught his attention, it passed, and he focused on what Dennis was sharing.

They continued their conversation into the parking lot as they made their way to their cars. After closing his car door and turning on the engine, John realized he'd left the paperwork from the city on the end table in Dennis's office. Because of the sensitivity of the information, he decided to head back inside to grab it so he could take it home.

He strolled back into the building, still feeling a high from all that had taken place with the zoning board. He looked forward to sharing the good news with Abigail. Immediately upon entering Dennis's office he found the papers. As soon as he had them in hand, he turned off the lights and closed the door behind him.

As he walked passed Dave's office, he noticed the door was cracked just a bit, so he decided to pop his head in to congratulate Dave again and encourage him to get home to celebrate with Beth. What he saw stunned him—a moment so surreal, he questioned if it was actually happening. The young lady who'd passed him in the hall earlier was in Dave's office and he was passionately kissing her. Apparently, they didn't think anyone was around at that time. When they saw John, the woman turned away from John's gaze and whispered in a barely audible voice, "I knew it was a mistake to meet you here." Dave's eyes met John's then he looked down in shame and silence. What could he say?

John stood there, breath shallow, hands clammy, frozen like a statue. His mind raced, grasping for a logical explanation but there was none. He had seen so many things in his career—corporate betrayals, broken promises—but nothing had prepared him for this. It was only a moment

Chapter 18 – From the Mountain Top to the Wilderness

but felt like an eternity to everyone. He barely noticed the young lady as she slipped past him and quickly made her way down the hall. His brain registered what happened, but his heart refused to accept it. Dave—his trusted friend—was potentially destroying the life he'd built with Beth and everything he, Dennis, and John had worked for, all for a moment of pleasure. Speechless, stunned, he turned and walked away—joy draining into grief with each step. From the mountaintop to the wilderness—joy to despair in a single moment. Because of her friendship with Beth, Abigail would be devastated too.

Despite the sadness and confusion, as he sat in his car staring out the window trying to process everything, a verse rose in his mind, "For all have sinned and fall short of the glory of God" (Romans 3:23). If ever there was a moment for grace, this was it. But how to extend it when his own heart felt betrayed?

> **Reflection:** Leadership often feels like a climb—each step a victory, each challenge a test. But the real test comes not on the mountaintop, but in the wilderness, when betrayal or failure shatters our expectations. In that moment, like John, we're faced with a choice: to react from pain or respond with grace. When someone falls, do we judge—or do we remember our own brokenness and offer the same mercy God gives us? In your wilderness moments, will you still choose grace?

Chapter 19 – Speaking the Truth in Love

"Nathan then said to David, 'You are the man!'"

—2 Samuel 12:7

John drove home in a daze. His hands gripped the wheel, eyes fixed ahead, a thousand thoughts seemed to hit him at once but on the other hand, nothing was registering. He stared straight ahead, driving home on autopilot. How do you process what just happened with someone you considered a friend and looked up to as a spiritual mentor? "Why, Lord?" repeated in his mind like a song playing on a loop inside his head

The situation gave John flashbacks to Bob McMillen, the CEO he worked for at MediTech. Like Dave, over time Bob had become both friend and mentor to John. Bob and his wife had done things socially with John and Abigail, so John was stunned when Bob's embezzlement was discovered. What had just transpired with Dave felt the same, but this was worse—more personal, more painful.

Abigail was in the kitchen fixing dinner when she heard John walk into the house. Knowing he was in the living room, she said loud enough to make sure he could hear, "How did the zoning meeting go? Did you and Joe get the final approval?" Her words didn't register. John sat, staring blankly out the window. Abigail repeated her question but not getting a response she walked into the living room and said, "John, I asked you a question."

"Huh?" was his only response.

Chapter 19 – Speaking the Truth in Love

Abigail walked around to the front of the couch and could immediately tell that something had happened. The distant look on John's face instantly filled her with dread that something awful, perhaps the death of someone in the family or a close friend, had taken place. "John, what's wrong?" she asked, with a concerned tone in her voice.

Grasping for words, John finally murmured, "I saw Dave kissing another woman in his office."

The look of shock on Abigail's face almost matched John's. While John had just formed a friendship with Dave, Abigail had known Beth and Dave for years. She was especially close to Beth because of church activities and participation in women's Bible studies. She knew Beth would be devastated. "John, I'm so sorry for you, and also for Beth."

"I've never faced something like this, so I have no idea what to do," he said, almost as if he were speaking to himself. "Do I confront Dave? Do I tell Beth? Should Dennis be brought in since Dave is an elder?" he muttered.

Abigail said, "I don't think there's a *right* answer, John. But I'm sure of this, before we take any steps, we need to pray about it. We need to ask God to show us the path to take."

Abigail said "we" because now she bore this burden too. Silence wasn't an option. What would she want someone to do for her if the tables were turned? Abigail knew she'd want a friend to tell her the truth, no matter how hard or hurtful, because she would not want to live a lie. Beth was her friend, and she owed that to her, but she had to balance that with the reality John was facing.

After much time in prayer, together and alone, they spent time talking about what they'd want someone to do for them if they faced the same situation. They decided they needed to confront Dave together before going to Beth or Dennis. They chose to do this together because of Abigail's knowledge of the situation and her relationship with Beth. John didn't regret bringing Abigail into the mix because he'd always leaned on her for advice, whether it was spiritual or business. For her part, Abigail wished she didn't know what she knew but was thankful that John confided in her rather than carrying the burden alone.

Later that evening, John texted Dave four words, "We need to talk." Knowing what it was regarding, but too embarrassed to meet at the church, Dave replied, "Can we meet at the coffee shop at 7:00 a.m. tomorrow?" John agreed then let him know that Abigail would be with him.

Dave was angry—and afraid. That Abigail knew terrified him. That Beth might find out? Even worse. He'd hoped to convince John it wasn't as big a deal as John thought. No matter how Dave was feeling or what he was thinking, he had little room to negotiate.

***

The next morning, John was up earlier than normal. He'd had difficulty sleeping and felt a little queasy in the pit of his stomach. As he looked in the bathroom mirror, he wondered why he felt so strongly about this situation, especially considering he'd only known Dave a relatively short time. He'd handled hard conversations before—but this was different. This betrayal hit close to home.

Shortly after John awoke, Abigail rolled out of bed. Their silence spoke louder than words as they dressed and got ready to meet Dave at the coffee shop. It was during this quiet time that John's mind wandered back to Paul. Paul was a MediTech trainee under John's care. John had to confront him regarding his drinking. He thought about his phone calls with his coach Duane Edwards and his friend Al Harris before speaking with Paul. The wisdom those two shared all those years ago would come in handy once again. Although Paul was let go from MediTech because of his drinking, he eventually turned his life around and thanked John for having the courage to confront him.

Abigail and John arrived early, hoping to steady themselves. But Dave was already there—waiting, unraveling. Seated at a table in the back corner, he looked as if he'd been there for quite a while. There were bags under his eyes, a clear indication he'd not slept, his hands wrapped around a cup of coffee that had gone cold. He'd arrived early, hoping to steady himself, but the minutes only made the dread settle deeper in his chest. His mind raced with excuses, justifications, half-truths he

Chapter 19 – Speaking the Truth in Love

might tell John and Abigail. But every scenario ended the same—with Beth finding out and his world unraveling.

He rose when the two made their way to the table but wouldn't look either directly in the eye. He was no longer the confident soldier John first met months ago for coffee with Dennis.

"Does anyone know how to start such a difficult conversation?" John thought to himself. Then he silently prayed, "Lord, you know. You know everything. You know Dave, his heart and his situation. Show us what to do."

John opened softly, "Dave, we love you. That's why we're here. If we didn't care about you and Beth, we would not put ourselves in such an uncomfortable position."

"I understand," was all Dave could muster in the moment.

"I'm sure you're not happy that Abigail is here but I know you're not shocked that I would confide in her as you've no doubt done with Beth over the years. We want to see you deal with whatever led you to make such a mistake. It's not our role to counsel or pry but to speak the truth in love. After praying about this, we know you need to tell Beth and Dennis."

Dave's voice grew loud as he protested, "I understand where you're coming from because I've had to deal with couples before, but this was one time, one kiss. Telling Beth will only make things worse." He was lying to John, Abigail, and himself, and he knew it.

Abigail was always so kind and loving that Dave had never seen her firm and uncompromising side. She politely said, "Dave, as a wife and mother, as well as Beth's close friend, I guarantee, she will want to know."

Dave's jaw stiffened and he could feel anger rising up, even though he knew she was right. Who were they to judge? But deep down, he knew—if Beth had done the same, he'd be devastated. That internal admission caused him to relax just a bit. He relented and said, "You're right. But I don't see any reason to involve Dennis."

John countered, "As an elder, you're expected to conduct yourself in a manner that's above reproach. You've not done that but more importantly, Dennis is the one who can help you navigate this to experience forgiveness, healing, and to hopefully save your marriage. This may seem small to you—but to Beth, it will be huge."

Again, Dave felt anger swelling but this time he didn't wait for it to pass. "I don't need a lecture on what it means to be an elder, John," he said forcefully.

Abigail and John had discussed whether or not they should go to Beth or give Dave a deadline. Either approach was risky. Last night Abigail asked John, "What if he doesn't tell her? What if he drags this out and Beth finds out from someone else?"

John sighed, exhaled and said, "I know. But if we go to Beth first, Dave might feel betrayed and completely shut down. If he's going to turn this around, he has to be the one to take responsibility." After some deliberation they agreed to give Dave the chance to tell Beth.

Unfazed by Dave's brief outburst Abigail didn't flinch, saying, "We know this will be hard but it's not our place to tell Beth or Dennis. That's your responsibility. However, if you don't do so in three days, we will approach Beth and Dennis. That's not a threat; it's accountability for your own good. We want to make sure you do the right thing for everyone involved."

It was clear to John and Abigail that Dave was not happy with their proposed next step. The old soldier was used to giving orders, not taking them. But what could he do? If he were on the battlefield in this situation, he'd know it was a lost cause to keep fighting and that the longer the battle dragged on, the more casualties and devastation there would be. No amount of justification or rationalization was going to work. John and Abigail were united—and unmovable. With no way out, and under the weight of conviction, Dave assured them he would speak with Dennis right away and then Beth before Friday afternoon.

John and Abigail stayed at the coffee shop for several minutes after Dave left. John's mind drifted to the community center. "What would happen if this got out? Would the project survive the fallout? Would the city council lose confidence? Would volunteers back out?" Influence wasn't just about moving forward—it was also about protecting the trusted relationships that had already been built.

Abigail broke the silence, "John, the project is in God's hands. What matters most right now is helping Dave and Beth find a way forward. If we do what's right, God will take care of the rest."

He knew she was right.

> **Reflection:** Influence isn't about avoiding hard truths—it's about loving people enough to speak to them. When John and Abigail confronted Dave, it wasn't to condemn—it was to call him back to truth, to healing, and to integrity. Love never ignores sin, but it also never withholds grace. Who in your life needs to hear the truth in love? And will you have the courage to speak—not to win, but to restore?

Chapter 20 – Waiting on the Lord

"Wait for the Lord;
Be strong and let your heart take courage;
Yes, wait for the Lord"

—Psalm 27:14

After meeting with Dave, all John and Abigail could do was wait—on Dave, and more importantly, on the Lord. They hoped Dave would be true to his word and confess to Dennis, and most importantly, to Beth. They both knew only the Lord could bring about healing in Dave and his relationship with Beth, but Dave needed to repent by taking the first steps.

John got confirmation the next day that Dave had spoken to Dennis because Dennis asked John to come to his office. Upon entering the spacious office, John closed the door behind him, took a seat, and Dennis followed suit.

"John, I'm not breaking any confidence when I tell you, Dave came to me and told me what happened with the young lady in his office. I share that because he also told me about his conversation with you and Abigail. Thank you for confronting the situation with so much grace and love. I do this for a living and it's never easy, so I'm sure it was extremely difficult for you and Abigail."

"Thanks Dennis." John's eyes welled up. He cleared his throat before speaking, the weight of it all pressing down. "As hard as that was, it's been more difficult thinking about Beth. We can't imagine how she will feel when she gets the news. Honestly, it's shaken my faith—more than I expected. I've come to see Dave as a friend and spiritual mentor these last several months."

"That's understandable, John. As you might imagine, I've seen more than my fair share of this during my career and it's never easy to process, especially with people in church leadership," Dennis said in an empathetic tone.

John innocently asked, "How do you get beyond it, thinking you know someone and wondering where the Lord is in all this?"

Dennis told him, "If David, a man after God's own heart, could fall so far, then none of us are beyond failure. And look at Peter; he swore on his life that he'd never deny Christ, but within 24 hours he did exactly that, three times. The Bible tells us Christ was tempted in all things as we are, but He's the only one who *never* caved to sin. We may not sin like David—but we're no less in need of grace. That's what we need to extend to Dave right now, so he turns back, just as Peter and David turned back to God. Perhaps in time God will use Dave in a mighty way just as he did with those two and so many others."

Once again, Scripture jumped off the page and into John's reality. The more he thought about the last two months with the community center project, the more he felt he was living a biblical story in real time. He'd experienced firsthand answers to his prayers in unmistakable ways. He'd seen God divinely arrange encounters with the right people at the right times. He was learning how the skill of influence he'd been blessed with had its foundation on scriptural principles. And now he could understand to some degree, the heartache Christ must have felt when people, especially His disciples, betrayed Him. Everything was moving from John's head to his heart—where true transformation takes place. It felt wonderful but ached at the same time. That too made him realize, with the diversity of humanity and our actions, both good and bad, God must feel joy, sorrow, love, anger, and every other emotion at the same moment, forever and always.

Dennis went on, "John, you said you felt Dave's been a mentor to you. He said the same about you. He told me he was amazed at your abilities and was learning from you as well. He said, as much as it hurt and angered him to have to talk with you and Abigail, he respected how you two handled everything. It won't be an easy road for him and Beth, but I'm confident they'll come through this together because of their love for the Lord, their love for each other, and the support of close friends. As bad as it is, never lose sight of this truth; God is much bigger than this situation. I have a feeling you and Abigail will play a significant role in their restoration."

"I know I speak for Abigail when I say, we'd be honored to be there for both of them," John replied.

Then Dennis shifted the conversation. He proceeded to tell John that he'd asked Dave to step down from his elder position. "If you're willing, I'd like to put your name forward to fill Dave's position as elder. The way you've led the project, and more importantly, how you've conducted yourself these last two months, I think the church would benefit from your presence. Of course, it would require a vote from the other elders."

John was flattered. The situation reminded him of what transpired when Bob McMillen was let go from MediTech for embezzlement. The board asked John to fill in as interim CEO. In neither case was John seeking positions of authority, but God was orchestrating the timing of everything. John sat in silence for a moment, feeling the weight of the offer. Leadership in business had been one thing, but spiritual leadership? That was different because it carried eternal weight. He wondered if he was ready to carry such a heavy burden.

"Dennis, early on I told you that I was seeking purpose since leaving MediTech. The fact that you see traits in me that give you confidence in me stepping into that role is both humbling and flattering. I'll need to talk this over with Abigail and get back to you, okay?" John had learned from his prior mistakes in his career to not jump on opportunities, no matter how good they might appear, without getting Abigail's blessing first. Dennis nodded in agreement.

True to his word, Dave confessed to Beth on Friday. As anyone might imagine, she was devastated. Beth didn't want him in the house, but Dennis advised against separation. If it had been a case of domestic

Chapter 20 – Waiting on the Lord

abuse, he would have insisted the abuser move out immediately and get professional help. However, when it came to infidelity, he'd seen times when people split for a period, and it usually didn't end well. That's so because it was too easy for the devil to creep in and sow more seeds of discord with both people. The longer couples stay apart, the harder it is to heal—and the easier it is for bitterness to take root. As difficult as it was for Beth to be around Dave because of the thoughts about what took place, she reluctantly agreed with Dennis's counsel. Everyone knew it would take a long time to rebuild trust, but they knew it wasn't impossible having seen other couples overcome much worse.

***

John sat down that evening with Abigail. "Dennis told me that he spoke to Dave and Beth," John told her. "He said it was one of the hardest conversations of his life because of his longstanding friendship with both."

"I've not spoken to Beth yet," she replied.

"I have something else to talk over with you." For several minutes he shared in detail what he and Dennis had discussed regarding the elder position. Despite the honor that was being offered to John, neither could celebrate given the circumstances.

"John, I'm so happy for you," she began, then went on, "but I can't rejoice right now knowing what led to it." She too recalled the situation with Bob McMillen because she'd done many things socially with his wife and enjoyed her company. The big difference this time was how personal it felt because she was much closer to Beth than she was to Mrs. McMillen.

"I always knew God had more for you," she said, "but I never imagined it would look like this."

"I'm right there with you," John replied. "Everyone would like to believe the call of God is a glorious, feel good thing, but I'm seeing that's often not the case. Even though David was anointed as the future king, he never rushed God's timing—and he grieved Saul's fall. I feel like that right now."

"I know you said this feels like a heavy burden," Abigail said. "Actually, it will be far too heavy for you if you lean on your own strength and understanding. But remember, Jesus said, 'My yoke is easy, and My burden is light.'" At that, John seemed to relax some.

As she looked at John, she was amazed at his transformation since leaving MediTech, especially these last few months. No more words were necessary. They knew what John had to do. Then they hugged and cried.

***

The following day John met with Dennis and told him about his conversation with Abigail, the honor they both felt about the offer, and their mixed emotions. While Dennis was also disappointed at how the offer for eldership came about, he felt confident about his decision to ask John to step into the role. He saw John's humility—this wasn't ambition, it was calling.

Then Dennis said, "John, I have one final thing to discuss. As you know, I had you working with Dave because of his position and knowledge regarding how things work in the church. It seems as though the toughest obstacles for the community project might be behind us now. Would you feel comfortable continuing to do what you're doing but reporting directly to me?"

John paused for a moment. He knew taking on the responsibility of being an elder and both roles around the project would be too much. "I think reporting directly to you would work but the tasks for the community center are still too much for one person." Then a thought occurred to John. In that moment, he wondered—was this another instance of divine inspiration? "I think I know someone who could step in to give us the help we need."

Dennis's curiosity was piqued, "Who do you have in mind?"

"Martha Cook," John replied.

Dennis's eyebrows raised, he smiled and nodded in agreement.

Reflection: Waiting on God doesn't mean doing nothing—it means trusting Him when the next step feels uncertain. John's journey reminds us that spiritual leadership is often born in trial, not triumph. When doors open in hard times, do we rush through—or wait on God's timing, prioritizing His guidance over our plans? As was the case with Moses, God often uses wilderness seasons to prepare us for sacred callings. Are you willing to wait—and to lead with humility when the call comes?

Chapter 21 – Anointed for Leadership

"Then Samuel took the flask of oil, poured it on his head, kissed him and said, 'Has not the Lord anointed you a ruler over His inheritance?'"

—1 Samuel 10:1

With Dave's blessing, Dennis informed the elders during their mid-week meeting to let them know Dave was stepping down from his roles as elder and leader of the community center project. He offered no specifics and people were sensitive enough not to pry. They trusted their pastor would share only what was necessary—and act wisely.

After the somber news, Dennis shifted gears to John and the vacant elder seat. He talked about John's work on the community center and his unmistakable answers to prayer along the way. He praised John's ability to win others over—inside and outside the church—with humility and grace. "I've never been more sure of God's anointing for someone to step into a leadership role than I am with John Andrews," he told the group.

By now, all the elders were familiar with John and the amazing progress he'd made on the community center. Dennis reminded them it took Nehemiah 52 days to rebuild the walls of Jerusalem, and that it was no coincidence that it took the church 52 days to get city approval. The building wasn't built, but people knew it was a small miracle to get the Clairemont city council and zoning board approval so quickly. A few questions followed, but with John's reputation and Dennis's

Chapter 21 – Anointed for Leadership

endorsement, no one objected. The group took a vote, and it was unanimous. John would be installed as an elder the following Sunday at the beginning of the first service.

***

Time seemed to be moving more rapidly than usual with all that had been happening at The Rock, and Sunday rolled around quickly. The sanctuary was filled with the buzz of conversation as people settled into their seats. Sunlight streamed through the stained-glass windows, casting a mosaic of colors on the walls. It felt like more than an ordinary Sunday. There was an air of expectancy, as if everyone knew something important was about to happen.

At Dennis's bidding, the elders made their way to the stage and stood in a semi-circle. Their expressions a mix of reverence and pride. They had been through seasons of blessing and hardship, and today felt like a turning point. John noticed a few nodding at him, silent affirmation of their support.

Dennis asked John and Abigail to join him and the elders. Standing on stage, John felt a wave of emotions. His mind drifted back to the first meeting with Dennis, Joshua handing out Gideon Bibles, and the days wrestling with his purpose. All of it had led to this moment, something he never expected, but was filled with gratitude for.

Dennis updated the congregation on the progress of the community center and John's pivotal role. As Dennis spoke, John saw Dave and Beth sitting near the aisle, a few rows from the back. When John's eyes met Dave's, Dave lowered his head, as if he were ashamed of the standing that he'd lost in the church due to his actions. It was like a demotion for the old soldier, only worse. Beth continued to look straight ahead, and Abigail noticed tears flowing down her cheeks. It was another moment of joy and sorrow wrapped into one for John and Abigail.

Dennis took the microphone, his voice steady but filled with emotion. "Today, we're not just filling an elder's seat. We are affirming God's calling on a man who has shown us what it means to lead with humility and serve with love. John Andrews didn't seek this role—it sought him, and that's how God works."

Dennis, looking at John, went on, "Just as Samuel anointed David, not for his outward appearance but for his heart, we are here today because we see God's heart in John. His journey with the community center has not just been about building walls and rooms—it's been about building bridges between people in this community."

The elders gathered around John and place their hands on him and Abigail. Everyone bowed their heads, and Dennis led the congregation in prayer, "Father, anoint John with wisdom and grace. May his leadership bring unity, his words bring healing, and his faith inspire others."

Almost to a person, everyone knew John because of his interaction with the congregation regarding how to finance the community center project. They appreciated his creativity to involve outside businesses and individuals as a solution to the financial stress many were feeling. Church was no different than business: there were some skeptics, but for the most part they were people who viewed everything with a critical eye. They liked to call themselves "realists," but in reality, they always saw the glass half empty rather than half full. Because most in the congregation knew this small contingent were full-time critics, they didn't sway others in their direction.

As people filed out of the sanctuary after the service, a woman approached John, her young daughter by her side. "Thank you for stepping into this role," she said. "We need leaders who listen and care." Her daughter shyly handed him a handmade card with crayon hearts and the words, "Thank you!!" scrawled across the front.

John thanked the woman and her daughter, then spotted Martha. He politely asked to dismiss himself because Martha was heading to the door, and he wanted to speak with her before she made her way into the parking lot. John had prayed about this conversation with Martha. Although she'd offered to review timelines in their previous conversation, this ask would be more significant. He knew he needed her skills, but more than that, he felt God nudging him to mend their relationship in a much deeper way.

Chapter 21 – Anointed for Leadership

"Martha, can I speak with you for a moment?" he asked.

She wasn't sure what to make of the encounter. While her opposition to the project had decreased, she was still feeling the sting of not having been chosen, and also a good bit of conviction for how she'd acted towards John. Nonetheless she said, "Sure, John. And congratulations on being installed as an elder."

As they made their way to a secluded area for some privacy, John replied, "Thank you, Martha."

Once they were away from everyone he said, "Believe me, I was as surprised as anyone when Dennis asked me. When he and I had that conversation, he also asked that I report directly to him on all things regarding the community center, basically taking on my role and Dave's. There's still so much to do and with Dave stepping away, I told Dennis I thought it would be too much for me to handle alone."

The look on Martha's face revealed she was a little surprised by that last statement. Surely a former CEO like John could handle a church project by himself she thought.

John went on, "Immediately you came to mind to come alongside me to help shepherd the project."

Martha was both stunned—and humbled. "John, why would you want me to work so closely alongside you after how I reacted to not being chosen in the first place?" she asked somewhat sheepishly but with sincere curiosity.

Then he asked her a question that seemed to come out of the blue. "Have you ever read, *Team of Rivals*?"

"I'm familiar with the title but I've not read the book," she replied.

"It's about the life of Abraham Lincoln and his election to the presidency. No one thought he had a chance and the three men he ran against in the primary—his rivals—thought it was a huge mistake that he was chosen as the nominee. Some even actively worked to undermine him. But once elected, Lincoln knew each possessed skills the country needed so he invited all of them into his cabinet."

Martha sensed where this was going as John continued, "I believe you're the right person—for this time, for this task. We've received approval from the city council and zoning board and now we have to start the hard work of making the building a reality. We need someone with strong project management skills to work with the construction company."

"But John, I wasn't very Christian-like in my response to you," she said half ashamed.

Undeterred he replied, "I appreciated your honesty in telling me how you really felt when we first met. I want people around me who will be that honest. I know you love this church and have worked tirelessly on behalf of it. That coupled with your project management background and financial acumen, make you the perfect person for the job. In fact, you were the only person who came to mind. So, would you be willing to work with me?"

Martha was flattered and a little embarrassed that John would approach the situation as graciously as he had. She'd not encountered people in her career who handled themselves that way. It was a bit overwhelming for her because she was still a little conflicted. She still had some lingering resentment to work through but desperately wanted to play a role on such an important project. John could see the internal struggle and noticed she was getting a little misty eyed as she got ready to respond. "John, you don't know how much this means to me. All I've wanted to do was help. I realize now that I pushed too hard. I guess old habits die slowly. I'm sorry for how I acted earlier."

"I understand, Martha. These past two months have taught me that ministry isn't corporate—but people are still people, and grace is always needed. Sometimes it's discouraging because I expected it to be different in a good way but that's not always the case. The biggest thing I've come away with so far is my need to integrate spiritual principles with the things I learned in the corporate world. As Paul encouraged us, we have to become all things to all people. In his case, he was winning souls. In our case, it's ethically influencing people for something that can have a similar eternal impact. I believe the community center will have that impact."

"John, it would be an honor to work alongside you on this," she said as she extended her hand.

Chapter 21 – Anointed for Leadership

Abigail watched from a distance, smiling as she saw Martha and John shaking hands. She knew John had influenced her to come on board but more importantly, that he'd won Martha over.

John and Abigail remained longer than normal in the lobby so they could give time to everyone who approached them. As the crowd thinned, John was shaking hands and sharing smiles when, across the room, he saw Martha talking with a few people. She smiled; her hands animated as she spoke—a rare display of enthusiasm. She saw John and nodded, a small gesture but one full of meaning. It felt like the first step on a new path—one they would walk together.

> **Reflection:** God doesn't call the qualified—He qualifies the called. John's anointing wasn't the result of ambition but obedience, and through his humility, others—like Martha—found redemption too. Leadership in God's kingdom is servanthood wrapped in grace, and reconciliation is often the truest mark of spiritual maturity. Who might God be calling you to serve with—even if the road began with resistance? Like John and Martha, perhaps God is preparing a partnership for something bigger than either could accomplish alone.

Chapter 22 – Influence Starts with Connection

"In the beginning was the Word,
and the Word was with God,
and the Word was God.
He was in the beginning with God."

—John 1:1–2

In the weeks that followed, Dave and Beth met with Dennis regularly. They were making progress, but it was slow going, similar to the feeling you have when you're staring at the clock waiting for the time to pass. Abigail was getting together with Beth, but Dave hadn't responded to John's attempts to connect, so John gave him space. For his part, Dave was not only dealing with his marriage, but he also started feeling resentment towards John. It wasn't that John had done anything wrong, it was just difficult for Dave to see John in the role he once occupied. Pain has a way of unearthing emotions that might otherwise stay buried.

John started meeting with Dennis consistently because of the community center but felt he needed more. He asked Dennis if he would mentor him. "Dennis, I know we're communicating regularly because of the community center but I'd like to ask for a little more of your time during these meetings." His mind wandered back to people who had been so helpful during his career; Duane, Ben, Franchesca, Russell, Nancy, and so many others who'd coached and mentored him. "Would you be willing to mentor me—more intentionally?" he asked.

Given John's background and his handling of everything up to this

Chapter 22 – Influence Starts with Connection

point, Dennis was a little surprised. "John, you seem to have a great handle on things. Sometimes I think I should be asking *you* to mentor me. What are you looking for from me?"

"Iron sharpens iron so maybe we can help each other," he replied. "I know a lot about leadership and people, but dealing with both in a church environment is quite a bit different than the business world."

Based on his decades as a pastor, Dennis readily agreed that it was. He said Dave learned that right away when he moved from the army to a civilian business and then into church work. Humans are humans in all cases but the expectations that different cultures create necessitates dealing with people differently.

Dennis leaned back in his chair. "John, you're right, leadership in the church is not like leadership in the corporate world. In business, success is often measured by growth and profit. Here, it's measured by spiritual maturity and the fruit that's produced in people's lives. No charts or spreadsheets for that. It takes time and patience, and God's timing is rarely ours."

John shared a struggle he was having with a skeptical church member. Dennis nodded, "When I first started here, I thought my job was to fix people. But I learned my role is to love them. Sometimes love looks like patience; sometimes it looks like truth spoken gently. It's rarely about having all the answers."

John absorbed everything Dennis shared that day, applying much of it to his relationship with Martha. He planned to meet with Martha weekly, similar to how he met with and coached his direct reports at MediTech. John had three goals with her: update her on the project, understand her better, and share the faith–influence connection he'd discovered.

***

Not long after meeting with Dennis, John had his first weekly meeting with Martha.

"Martha, as a project manager, I'm pretty certain getting people to say yes and stay on track was one of your top priorities," he said one morning when they met at The Coffee House.

"After knowing how to assess a project and then laying out the plans, that was probably number one," she said as she sipped her cappuccino.

"What kind of training did you get during your career that helped you in that area," he innocently inquired.

She chuckled, "None. When I started, you were left to figure it out for yourself or, if you were lucky, you'd learn from someone who seemed to know what they were doing."

John leaned back in his chair, sighed and said, "Unfortunately, that's been the case for nearly everyone I've met. We're trying to influence people every day, so people mistakenly think they naturally know how to do it. I think in my career, the biggest success factor was recognizing that influence is a skill and that there's a science to it, which means it can be studied, taught, and learned."

"That never occurred to me. Truthfully, when people talked about influence, persuasion, and communication, I thought it was just motivational hype," was her candid reply.

"I took a psych class my freshman year of college that touched on the science of influence. When I tried some of the approaches the course outlined, and saw how effective they were, I decided to keep learning and trying new approaches. Now here's the really cool thing—I'm beginning to see how these principles have their roots in Scripture," he said with an animated tone that caught Martha's attention.

"I have some time before I need to talk with the contractor about our building plans. Give me a quick preview," she told him in a businesslike tone of voice.

"Absolutely! These are principles I'd like to spend a little time on whenever we get together because I think they'll help you shepherd the project along with more ease," he said as he put his coffee mug down. He leaned in and went on, "Let's start with the principle of liking. I'm sure you already know this—if people like you, they're more inclined to say yes to you."

"That's kind of a no-brainer, John. I think everyone knows that," Martha replied.

John smiled because he'd heard that many times in the past. "Here's

Chapter 22 – Influence Starts with Connection

the thing; most people go about it wrong. They spend so much time trying to get people to like them that it repels people. It reminds them of a desperate salesperson. The key is this—don't focus on getting people to like you. Focus on genuinely liking them. It's a small change that can lead to big differences. Think of it a little like love, looking for the best in others, even if they don't deserve it."

Martha was clearly thinking about what John had just shared. "That makes sense but honestly, I never invested much in work relationships. We had jobs to do, not friendships to build. If we clicked, great. If we didn't, that was okay too because we were paid to do the job, not make friends," she said in a matter of fact tone.

"I get it Martha but I'm telling you, tapping into the principle of liking can make a huge difference because of what it does for *you*. Be honest, don't you find yourself working harder, longer, and more creatively for people you like than those you don't?" She couldn't deny that.

He went on, "The icing on the cake is that you'll enjoy the people you work with much more when you approach this principle with the right mindset."

She furrowed her brow as she thought about all that John had shared. "Okay, I've got a few more minutes. Give me another one of your psychological tricks."

John's tone shifted, "Martha, they're not tricks, they're principles all humans live by. I know you wouldn't like it if you learned someone used a 'trick' on you to get you to do something. Words matter. Remember, 'In the beginning was the Word, and the Word was with God, and the Word was God,'" he said, citing the opening from the Gospel of John.

Having been a churchgoer a good part of her adult life, Martha was a tad embarrassed when she realized what she'd said. "You're right. Sorry for the sarcasm."

He smiled knowing he was getting through to her. "The other principle I'll share with you is called reciprocity."

"Favor trading," she chimed in.

"Not exactly. Reciprocity is the natural obligation we feel to give back to someone who first gives to us. But it's not a give to get mentality.

Jesus didn't give to get; He gave freely because He loved. If we utilize the principle of liking correctly, we'll naturally want to help those we consider friends. It moves giving from transactional to relational. The good news is most people you form a relationship with and help with a sincere heart will want to help you when you need it. Surely you remember, 'Give, and it will be given to you' (Luke 6:38), and 'He who sows sparingly will also reap sparingly, and he who sows bountifully will also reap bountifully' (2 Corinthians 9:6). Those, and many other scriptures, show that reciprocity is a timeless principle God uses to get us to give as He does. Make sense?"

Martha was an analytical person by nature. It was a big reason she had excelled as a project manager throughout her IT career. Like so many people, she separated her work from her faith. It wasn't that she was opposed to it. She'd been taught that faith was private, not something to be shared at work. But more important than that, no one had ever connected faith and work for her like this. "John, what you're sharing holds a lot of interest but I'm not sure I'm where you are with all of this."

"I appreciate your honesty. I wouldn't expect you to see things the way I do after one conversation," he said as he laughed. "What I'm sharing with you I've been processing most of my adult life, and only recently have I begun to see the influence and faith connection."

They grabbed their empty coffee cups, dropped them in a bin with other dirty items, and began to make their way to the door. "Martha, same time next week?"

"Wouldn't miss it, John. You've got me thinking so I look forward to learning more," she replied.

John said, "Martha, next time, coffee's on me. It's the least I can do after subjecting you to all this influence talk."

Martha chuckled, "Deal. But only if you promise not to turn it into a lesson on reciprocity."

That brought a smile to John's face, a small but important step toward friendship. As they exited the building he said, "If you need me before next week, don't hesitate to reach out."

Chapter 22 – Influence Starts with Connection

With that, they went their separate ways. There were lots of people to meet with and new tasks to be tackled now that they were about to break ground on the community center.

As Martha drove home, she thought deeply about what John had shared. A bit jaded, she'd always thought influence was just a form of manipulation, a game played by those who wanted to control people and outcomes. But the way John described it—loving first, giving first—it sounded more like ministry than management. She wasn't ready to embrace it fully—but something in her spirit was stirring.

> **Reflection:** The best influence approach starts not with persuasion—but with presence. John's willingness to invest in Martha, without pressure, mirrors Christ's approach to discipleship: patient, personal, rooted in love. Influence, when separated from self-interest, becomes ministry. Where in your life are you trying to influence? Could a shift from "getting results" to "building relationships" transform the way others respond—and the way you lead?

Chapter 23 – Sowing and Reaping

"Give, and it will be given to you. They will pour into your lap a good measure—pressed down, shaken together, and running over. For by your standard of measure it will be measured to you in return."

—Luke 6:38

Martha dove into the project with the energy of an actor stepping into the spotlight on opening night. She felt an adrenaline rush much like she did during her career when she was assigned a new project to lead. It was her first real challenge since retiring, and she welcomed it. This was much different than any IT project she'd worked on, but she felt up to it and was excited by the challenge it presented.

After surveying the community center plans and proposed timeline, she was brimming with ideas. Once she felt she had her mind around everything she set up her first meeting with the general contractor. She was eager to help the community center to come into existence, but if she were honest with herself, it was just as important to her to prove herself to Dennis and John.

Martha met with Bob Holmes, the site supervisor for KDL Construction on the project. As they walked the plot of land that would house the community center, she decided to try some of John's relationship building advice. It was new for her, so she felt a little awkward as she started the conversation, "Bob, tell me a little about yourself and the company."

Bob was a bit gruff as you might expect from someone who was a career construction worker. Although he wasn't used to such questions

Chapter 23 – Sowing and Reaping

from the client, he proceeded to share a little about his family and career history.

Martha learned he was in his early 40s, although he looked a good bit younger than his age, and had two teenage boys. While he'd been in the construction industry his entire adult life, he freely admitted this was his first time being in charge of such a big project from start to finish. That concerned Martha—but realizing they were both in uncharted territory gave her an idea. She used it as a connection point. "Bob, it looks like this is a first for both of us. I managed projects throughout my career but never a building, so it looks like we'll both have some on the job training."

Her honesty relieved Bob a little. "I guess we're both coming in with some experience but in different ways," he said.

Martha replied, "No bad habits to overcome and perhaps we'll bring new perspectives to the project."

He chuckled and nodded at that statement.

"Bob, because you said this is your first time leading a project of this size, what do you think will be your biggest challenge?" Martha asked, genuinely curious.

Bob hesitated for a moment because it felt like he would be admitting a weakness. However, because he was starting to feel comfortable with Martha he said, "Honestly, it will be the paperwork. I'm used to being hands-on, swinging the hammer, not filling out forms."

Martha smiled, "I get that because it was a challenge I faced when I first started leading projects. Maybe I can help with the admin side—I've managed my share of paperwork-heavy projects, so I know how overwhelming all the details can be."

"I'd appreciate that," he replied with a hint of enthusiasm.

Then she switched to a more personal question, "Are you a resident of Clairemont?"

"No, but we don't live far away," he shared.

"You said you have a couple of teenagers. Do you think they'd be interested in coming to the community center?" she inquired.

He was impressed with her listening skills and genuine desire to get to know him. "We're not religious people but I think because of my involvement, the whole family might come over from time to time," Bob said as he looked around. Much like an artist staring at a blank canvas before putting the first brush stroke on it, he was beginning to envision what the place might look like once construction was completed.

Thinking about John's explanation of reciprocity, Martha asked, "Bob, given my background, is there anything else I can help you with to make this first project of yours go a little smoother?"

He appreciated the question and began to share more ideas on how she might help him. Then he asked her the same question, a natural response to reciprocity, and she shared a few thoughts.

Martha actually found herself enjoying the conversation. "Perhaps John is right about his communication philosophy," she thought to herself. The meeting concluded and she felt very good about what had been discussed and getting to know Bob.

***

In the meantime, John continued to meet with individuals and business owners about coming alongside the church in the building project. It wasn't only about raising funds for the construction phase. The ongoing operating expenses would be significant and require long-term commitments. He knew from his sales days how to go about the ask. He started with the building fund. That's where the most money would be needed initially. Start with the big ask because you might just get it but if not, always be ready with fallback positions you can lay on the table during the same meeting. He remembered the old axiom, "Anticipating no is not pessimistic, it's strategic because it allows you to think through your fallback positions." It was an application of reciprocity by way of concession.

He met with Kurt Miller, the founder of a large temp service in town. Ease of Business supplied IT workers for projects that needed help but didn't need to bring on new full-time employees. Ease of Business was a big IT service provider for companies in the Charlotte and Raleigh

Chapter 23 – Sowing and Reaping

metro areas. MediTech had used them on numerous occasions, so John and Kurt had known one another for many years. The company also provided cloud storage for small businesses that didn't have the capacity or skillset to do it on their own.

They met in Kurt's office, which some might describe as somewhat spartan in appearance. Kurt kept a close eye on the bottom line, and he reasoned that so few people actually worked at the office that he should do all he could to minimize costs so he could pass the savings on to his customers.

"Kurt, great to see you again. Thanks so much for taking time to meet with me," John opened.

"My pleasure," Kurt said as they shook hands. "How's retirement treating you, John?"

"To be honest, I was getting a little bored. I know many people would envy the position Abigail and I are in, but I felt like I needed more than relaxation and vacations."

"I don't know, it sounds pretty good to me!" Kurt exclaimed with a grin.

"I would have said the same thing a few years ago, but once I was into it, I felt I needed a sense of purpose again. That's why I'm here today." Then John briefly shared what had transpired at The Rock, the vision Dennis had for the community center project, and his involvement. Next, he let Kurt know about the potential benefits for businesses that invested in the project. To engage social proof, he mentioned some of the businesses that had already committed. John knew Kurt would recognize most of the names because Ease of Business had supported many of them.

"Kurt, we're still looking for businesses and individuals to come alongside us on this project. I know you run a tight ship because it helps to keep costs down for your clients, but is there any room in your budget to help fund this project?" he inquired.

"John, everything you've shared is compelling, but I have to be honest, given the current state of the economy, many of our clients are scaling back. I can't afford any big cash outlays at this time," Kurt said, knowing he'd disappoint John.

"I get it, Kurt and understand how you feel," John replied. "I've spoken with lots of people the last few months and everyone is feeling the pinch. However, if it's not in the budget to fund the project up front, would you be open to a smaller, ongoing commitment to help with the monthly operational expenses? Every dollar helps, and it could be something you work into your monthly budget," John proposed in a relaxed tone so there would be no pressure on Kurt.

At that, Kurt looked up to his left. John could tell Kurt was doing the math in his head. After a short pause Kurt said, "I tell you what John, I'm grateful that you brought our people into MediTech all those years ago. We'd not been in business too long, so it really helped us get going. And, once other businesses knew we were working with you, it gave us lots of credibility. Could we start at $1,500 a month then revisit the commitment after a year?"

"I'm glad MediTech was able to be a part of your initial success, Kurt. That monthly commitment would be fantastic. Thank you so much," John exclaimed. He knew this small step tapped into the principle of consistency, which might make it easier for Kurt to commit to other ways he could help in the future. John wouldn't need to press Kurt because he was confident Kurt would see the benefits of the community center. That could come in the form of subtle advertising or perhaps finding young talented people who might want to work for Ease of Business in the future. On top of that, he would begin to see himself as an advocate.

After the two spent a little more time reminiscing and catching up they concluded the meeting. As John drove to his next appointment, he thought about how so many things led to that moment with Kurt. His decision to do business with Kurt and Ease of Business while running MediTech kickstarted their relationship and engaged reciprocity. Back then, John hadn't known how that decision would sow seeds for this moment—but God did. It reminded him of the late Zig Ziglar, a world-renowned author, trainer, and motivational speaker, who would encourage audiences to engage in reciprocity whenever he said, "You can get everything you want in life, *if* you will just help enough others get what they want."

Chapter 23 – Sowing and Reaping

Reflection: What you sow today, you may reap tomorrow—in ways you never expected. John's journey shows that ethical influence bears fruit over time. Authentic leadership is never about manipulation; it's about building trust, giving first, and meeting needs. Are there relationships or actions you've invested in that might, in God's timing, bring blessing and impact? As you sow seeds of kindness, wisdom, and grace, trust that God is orchestrating things you cannot see or imagine.

Chapter 24 – A Revelation

"You meant evil against me, but God meant it for good in order to bring about this present result."

—*Genesis 50:20*

Construction on the community center was well underway. Ground was broken weeks earlier in a small ribbon cutting ceremony. The crisp morning air was filled with a sense of anticipation and excitement, and the occasional laughter of children. Red and white ribbons fluttered in the breeze, and the gold-plated scissors gleamed in the sunlight as Dennis, John, and Martha officially cut the ribbon.

In addition to church members, several people from the city council and zoning board were present as were many of the business owners who'd offered financial support. A television crew from a local station even stopped by.

John scanned the crowd, hoping to see Victoria. He'd made headway getting to know her but more than that, despite not supporting the initiative, he thought she would make an appearance because she was a politician. He wondered if it was a final act of defiance on her part.

Stan Letterman was also in attendance, and afterwards he asked to interview Dennis and John. Projects like this were always a big deal in Clairemont so it would be front page news. John made sure to include Martha in the conversation. He understood how important it would be for her and, as overseer of the construction, she could best answer Stan's detailed questions. She beamed at the opportunity and John could see

Chapter 24 – A Revelation

why she had had such a successful career. She answered every question with confidence, adding rich details.

***

John continued to meet with Victoria. With her opposition now in the rearview mirror, their conversations took on a different tone. Always a bit of a skeptic, she was surprised that John continued to make it a point to reach out to have coffee with her, especially after her slight by not attending the ribbon cutting ceremony. She knew he didn't need anything from her at this point and appreciated his sincerity. However, she still had reservations about his possible future motives. Old habits and thought patterns die hard.

Instead of meeting at her office this day, they met at The Coffee House. It was a rainy morning as John made his way inside. He stood near the door, shaking his umbrella to get the rain off it when Victoria walked in.

As they made their way to a table, coffee in hand, she said in a formal tone, "John, I saw Stan's article about the ribbon cutting ceremony. Congratulations."

John knew she wasn't happy about it because she still felt like she'd lost. He was perplexed that she wasn't able to let it go by this time. "Thanks, we're excited about the impact it will have on the kids and volunteers." He made sure to mention the kids because, despite her resistance, Victoria did have a heart for children.

Through the grapevine she'd caught wind of why Dave had stepped away from the project, so she decided to press John on that. "It's come to my attention that Dave had to step away because of some indiscretion," she said, dropping it on the table like a hand grenade.

John was caught off guard by her bluntness. "Victoria, I would never share details of our conversations with anyone and in the same way, I don't talk about others," he said in a strong, serious tone Victoria hadn't heard him use before.

Nonetheless, she enjoyed a challenge, so she pressed him, "So, it's true."

John didn't take the bait. "I didn't say that, Victoria. My refusal to talk about Dave is out of respect for him. I'm treating him the way I would treat you or anyone else."

Victoria was getting frustrated. Her hands began to grip her coffee mug tightly, then she said, not realizing how much the tone of her voice betrayed her feelings, "If you ask me, churches are full of hypocrites."

John smiled. "No denial there, Victoria. I can't speak for anyone else, but I'll tell you that I'm a hypocrite. I don't always live up to my own beliefs and values, let alone God's. I'm thankful for His grace and forgiveness."

"I wasn't talking about you," she countered, in much the same way people do when they make derogatory statements about people groups, not realizing someone from the group is part of the conversation.

"Maybe not, but I'm far from perfect. Any good you see in me is because of God," he gently replied.

Thoughts of her father flooded her mind as she thought about what she'd heard about Dave. In a moment of anger and vulnerability, before she realized it, she blurted out, "My father cheated on me and my mom. He got up and left us without a word. This whole town thought he was a good, God fearing man, but he was just a hypocrite."

John sat there in amazement at what she'd just revealed. This wasn't a hand grenade; it was a bomb. After a moment of silence, he simply said, "Victoria, I'm so sorry that happened to you and your mother." What more could he say?

The rain was gently tapping on the window next to their table. Looking away because she didn't want John to see the hurt on her face, Victoria's voice softening momentarily, she said, "You've no idea how bad that hurt us. He used to call me his shadow because I was always with him. Then suddenly he was gone."

To John, her father's departure wasn't just abandonment—it was like a death, only worse because it was a choice. "You're right, I will never understand the depth of your hurt. Despite that, I do feel some of your pain. I'm a father so I know how much children look up to their parents, especially fathers. We're representatives of God in the eyes of our small children."

Chapter 24 – A Revelation

By now a few tears were on her cheeks and John could see, even with her head turned to look out the window. His whole being felt for her. "I wish there were something I could say or do that would alleviate some of your pain. What you're experiencing is almost like the death of a loved one. Only God could carry that kind of pain—and offer comfort in its place," he said in an empathetic tone.

"If God didn't want me to feel this pain, then He wouldn't have allowed my father to leave," she replied in an angry tone, her voice getting louder.

Trying to ease the emotional tension John said, "God never forces us to do anything. Your father made an awful choice and you're paying a heavy price for it. But God understands betrayal, and so does His Son."

He wasn't trying to reason Victoria out of how she was feeling. He hoped she would see that God does understand our pain, and more importantly, her pain.

She sat silent for a moment, trying to compose herself, hoping no one in the coffee shop noticed her.

John continued, "I know you went to church growing up so I'm sure you remember hearing this scripture, 'Blessed are those who mourn, for they shall be comforted.' That never did much for me until I came across a paraphrase from *The Message*, 'You're blessed when you feel you've lost what is most dear to you. Only then can you be embraced by the One most dear to you.'"

He paused for a moment and could see Victoria was still listening, so he went on. "When I think about that passage, it reminds me of our kids when they were little. If we gave one of them a new toy, it was their whole world. If they lost it or it broke, they'd come running to me or Abigail in tears. That's where they found comfort, in our arms. I think that's the picture God wants us to see. If you go to Him, He's faithful and you will find rest and comfort in His arms."

For the first time, Victoria found herself speechless—not from anger, but from the weight of truth. She'd not thought about it until now, but she'd never gone to God except in anger since her father left. It's hard to receive anything good from another person, let alone God, when you're blinded by anger. She said, "John, why do you even give a damn about me—or my father? You got your building project."

"As I told you when we first spoke, no matter what happened with the community center, or anything else in the future, I wanted to get to know you. I hope time has shown you that I was sincere when I said that. Perhaps what's unfolding was meant to be," he told her, hoping she might be open to the possibility.

"Meant to be?!" she exclaimed, the hurt in her voice still evident to John and loud enough now that a few people sitting nearby heard and turned to see what was going on.

Before she could say anything else, John said, "Joseph's brothers sold him into slavery, but when they realized who he was, and were afraid of the consequences of their actions, Joseph told them, 'You meant evil against me, but God meant it for good in order to bring about this present result.' Perhaps all of this—the community center, your resistance, and you and I forming a friendship—has been part of God's plan to help you come back to Him and ultimately forgive your father."

Victoria was stunned, as was John, at how everything was unfolding. Neither he nor Victoria had any idea this was the turn their conversation would take on this rainy day. She replied, "I didn't come here for a counseling session."

John sat there, not knowing how to respond.

Abruptly, she stood up. "I need to go." She grabbed her belongings and quickly made her way to the door without another word. John knew better than to go after her. He was overwhelmed by what had just taken place so he knew she must be reeling from the revelation God had given him to share. He sat there silently for several minutes, processing all that had just happened. He prayed a familiar prayer, "God, You know. You know Victoria's situation and her heart. Thank you for what just took place."

Reflection: God can use anything, especially our brokenness, to lead us back to Him—and to others. Victoria's anger masked years of pain, but in a single moment, God used John's gentleness to reveal truth and invite healing. Like Joseph, we all carry wounds caused by others, yet God's grace can transform our past into purpose. Is there a relationship in your life where compassionate presence might open the door to healing and reconciliation? Sometimes, simply showing up is all God requires of us—and He will do the rest.

Chapter 25 – Doubt to Clarity

"Walk with the wise and become wise, for a companion of fools suffers harm."

—Proverbs 13:20

Weeks had passed since John and Victoria's emotional meeting at The Coffee House. Despite her initial resistance to him and the project, and her sometimes standoffish nature, John knew that behind the exterior was someone worth befriending. Because of his concern for her, he reached out by phone and email but got no response. John's mind flashed back to Paul again, the MediTech trainee he'd once mentored. After Paul's DUI arrest, John reached out to him but never heard back. He trusted God was at work in Paul's life, which John found out in a very memorable way. Years later, John had unexpectedly bumped into Paul at a hospital in Seattle—a moment that reminded him God wastes nothing. That "chance" encounter he came to realize was another pivotal God moment in his life.

He decided the best approach with Victoria was to give her space as he'd done with Paul. He hoped in time they would reconnect but, just as it was in God's hands with Paul, so it was with Victoria.

***

John met with Martha at The Coffee House on Monday morning, and it was busier than usual. There was a long line as baristas worked behind

Chapter 25 – Doubt to Clarity

the counter like bees in a hive. Everyone knew their role and they were operating at maximum efficiency. All the tables would soon be occupied and there was the familiar buzz of casual conversation. John overheard more than one table talking about the community center. Between the newspaper article and television report on the groundbreaking ceremony, everyone knew about it.

Martha grabbed her cappuccino and made her way to the table where John was seated. He was delighted that she initiated the conversation by talking about her experience putting into practice what she'd learned from him regarding liking and reciprocity.

As she stirred her cappuccino, Martha leaned in, "John, I was skeptical about the relationship-building stuff—but I have to admit, it worked like a charm. Bob and I established instant rapport. I think it was mostly due to the fact that the community center is his first big project as a site supervisor and my first project of this type. We quickly realized we can support one another."

"That's great to hear, Martha!" John said enthusiastically. "Was there anything that stood out?"

"Something that caught my attention was, after asking how I could support him, unprompted he asked how he could support me. I doubt that would have stood out had you not explained reciprocity to me," she told John.

"Once you learn the language of influence," John said, "you start seeing it everywhere. It reminds me of Jesus talking about spiritual principles, when he told his followers, 'Otherwise they would see with their eyes and hear with their ears.' Most people miss influence."

He could see Martha was thinking so he went on with a more tangible example, "It's similar to buying a new car. When you drive it off the lot, don't you feel like you suddenly see your car everywhere?"

"Now that you mention it, I do. I bought a new car just over a year ago and began to notice it every time I was on the road," she replied.

"The only thing that changed was your perception. You began to notice something that had always been there, but you weren't seeing it. That's kind of how the principles of influence work; the more you learn, the more you notice them. Speaking of the principles, do you have time to learn a little about two more?" he inquired.

"Lay 'em on me," she said emphatically.

"Great relationships are important but not necessarily enough to always get what you need. Sometimes people like you a lot, but they're not sure what they should do. The principles of authority and social proof can be used to dispel uncertainty and instill trust and confidence," he began as he sipped his coffee.

"You mean like expertise and peer pressure?" Martha asked, confident she already understood.

"Sort of but not exactly," John told her. "Let's start with authority. To be considered a legitimate authority you need expertise *and* credibility. If you're missing either you won't be considered an authority."

"Makes sense but I never thought about the credibility part," she said with some curiosity in her voice. "I remember a project early in my career, I had the credentials but not the confidence. My team doubted me because I wasn't upfront about what I didn't know. It turned into a disaster. I can see now that admitting where I needed help might have earned me more trust and respect."

"It won't matter how much someone knows if you can't trust them, right?" he asked.

"Absolutely," she immediately replied. "I think we've all heard countless stories about people who used their expertise to take advantage of unsuspecting people," she said, remembering Bernie Madoff's multi-billion-dollar Ponzi scheme that hurt so many people.

John continued, "Early in my career there was a senior executive who had all the expertise in the world, but he lost his credibility when he routinely failed to follow through on promises. People stopped listening to him, and it became almost impossible for him to lead effectively. It was a powerful reminder that true authority isn't just about knowledge—it's also about integrity."

Martha nodded in agreement. It was a sad reality; one she'd seen all too often in her long career.

"And it won't matter how much you trust someone if you know they're not an expert, right?" he asked.

"Now I get it," she answered. "I love my parents, and trust them implicitly, but I don't want either doing surgery on me," she said with a chuckle.

"Exactly!" John said. He went on, "Jesus is our model for perfect authority. Despite having no formal title, money, or power, He changed the world. As the author of life, He knows what's best for us, so we should listen to Him. And, because He did what He asks us to do, following the will of His Father perfectly, we can trust Him."

"I know Bob sees me as an authority but won't building trust take time?" she inquired.

John set his half empty coffee mug on the table. "You're right. Building trust takes time but there are two things you can do to speed it up. First, let your 'yes' be yes and your 'no' be no. In other words, make sure you keep your word. Second, if you're wrong or aren't sure about something, be humble and admit it. Too many people try to 'fake it till they make it' and everyone can see through that," he shared.

"I know what you mean about people trying to fake it. I saw that plenty in my career and it was hard to rely on people when I clearly knew their knowledge was lacking," she replied.

"Martha, you've managed multimillion-dollar IT projects. Those experiences give you a unique perspective. Don't be afraid to share those stories with Bob. It's not about boasting—it's about showing him why your guidance can help this project to succeed," John encouraged her.

"Let's move on to social proof. Peer pressure is an application of social proof but in a negative way. It's easy and natural for us to follow the lead of others, especially those we see as similar to ourselves. However, we don't want our kids following the lead of other kids when it comes to things like drinking, drugs, or sex, so we warn them about peer pressure. Jesus did something similar when he said in Matthew, 'The gate is wide and the way is broad that leads to destruction, and there are many who enter through it' (Matthew 7:13)."

"Oh, I had those talks with my boys," Martha said, rolling her eyes. "They thought I was overprotective—until life proved me right," she said with a hint of satisfaction in her voice.

"I think my kids thought the same about me and Abigail until they became adults," John replied. "We can also use social proof to point people in the right direction and to right behaviors. Proverbs encourages us to 'Walk with the wise and become wise' (Proverbs 13:20). In your case, working with Bob, an example might be sharing what other builders or community centers do that works well. When people come in contact with information like that, most think, 'If it worked for them, it would probably work for me too.'"

"What other examples can you share with me," Martha asked with genuine curiosity.

Pleased with Martha's openness to learning, John went on. "Again, Jesus is our best example. Crowds followed Him, and the crowds drew more people—social proof in action."

Martha was busy taking notes, so he decided to share a final example, this one from his MediTech days. "Something that worked well during my career was to get vocal advocates on board *before* presenting a new idea. I made sure to win over not only senior leaders, but also informal leaders. When people knew respected peers were on board, it became much easier for others to come alongside."

"Not only did I get a free cup of coffee, but you also gave me food for thought," Martha joked.

John laughed. Their relationship had turned a corner—not just professionally, but personally—and he was grateful for it. He could clearly see that Martha was exceptionally good at her trade and he appreciated her quit wit.

With the construction well under way, there was lots Martha needed to attend too. For his part, John continued his outreach. Between the church pledges and funds from local business leaders they had reached their goal for the actual construction. With construction funded, John turned his focus to securing operating funds, setting guidelines, and assembling volunteers.

Chapter 25 – Doubt to Clarity

Reflection: As Martha's heart shifts from skepticism to confidence, we see how gentle, persistent leadership rooted in love can foster real transformation. Influence is never about control—it's about inviting and informing others into growth and partnership. John's patient guidance reflects the way Christ walks with us: offering truth, trust, and space to respond. The disciples didn't "get it" right away so be patient with people. Where might you be called to invest in someone's growth—not with pressure, but with presence and purpose?

Chapter 26 – A Good Deed?

*"Trust in the Lord and do good.
Dwell in the land and cultivate faithfulness."*

—Proverbs 37:3

Later that week, at 7:45 a.m., John received a call from Thomas May. John was in his office, coffee in hand, reviewing donor lists and planning his next outreach. Abigail was in the kitchen preparing breakfast, and the smell of bacon filled the first floor. They liked to eat together when their schedules permitted, which happened with more frequency since John's retirement.

"John, sorry to bother you so early but we have a major problem," Thomas said in a matter of fact tone, getting right to the point.

The Rock had received city and zoning approval so John couldn't imagine what the issue might be. Straightening up and leaning forward, matching Thomas's tone, John said, "Thomas, I can tell from your tone of voice this is serious. What's going on?"

Thomas began to share. "There's been a challenge filed in court over the deed to the land that you're building on."

John's stomach tightened and his hands suddenly felt clammy. "How could that be? We have a legitimate deed. The city knows that," John countered.

"That plot of land goes back to the 1840s when a family, the Allens, owned it. A distant relative is contending the land wasn't properly sold in the 1890s to the Smiths, the family The Rock purchased it from three years ago."

Chapter 26 – A Good Deed?

"I still don't understand," John said. "The Smiths had been on that land for over 100 years. How could something like this pop up all of a sudden?"

Thomas responded, "These days, people dig into ancestry for fun—and sometimes, it unearths complications. The person who filed the claim traced their family tree back to the Allens. They're contending there's a story that's been passed down in the family that the land was never actually sold. As the story goes, the family was unlawfully scammed out of the land."

John stood up and walked to the window, looking out at the neighborhood he and Abigail loved so much. The idea that this project could be derailed over a century-old land dispute was something no one could have anticipated. "Do you think there's any merit to it, Thomas?"

Thomas countered, "It doesn't matter what I think, John. Because a challenge has been filed in court, we need to look into it."

John felt his old CEO persona come to the surface. He'd been a problem solver, and this was a problem that needed to be solved ASAP. "What do we have to do to correct this?" John asked.

"Unless we can prove the land was rightfully purchased, the church will either have to buy or lease it from the person who is contending the deed. And that's contingent on them not wanting the land for some other use. It might be difficult to prove the sale was legit because who knows what records we still have. The sale to the Smiths took place more than 130 years ago."

"What should we do right now?" John asked.

"For the time being, sit tight and let me look into it," Thomas told him.

"Should we keep going with the building or stop until we hear from you?" John asked.

"At this point there's not a court order to stop you from proceeding with the construction but I have to tell you, it's a gamble. You'll need to decide," Thomas told him, trying to play it safe as any politician would.

"Thomas, thank you for the call. I'll talk with Dennis, and we'll decide what to do next. Any time you find out more information, please call me, no matter what time of day," John encouraged him.

"Will do," Thomas promised as they hung up.

John's heart and mind were racing. His first thought was that Victoria might be behind this.

Could she really go this far?

He hated that the thought even crossed his mind but given her opposition to the project and their emotional exchange the last time they met at The Coffee House, he knew anything was possible. She was shrewd and resourceful. If anyone could dig up some obscure legal challenge to stall the community center, it was her.

His hand hovered over the phone as he thought about calling her. Then he realized, if she wasn't behind it, the trust he'd built with her would be lost in an instant. He was between the proverbial rock and a hard place. He folded his hands, closed his eyes, and prayed in the manner that Jesus had taught his disciples.

"Father, You are everywhere and know everything.
You're completely separate and different,
Yet always with me and understand me.
No name and no words can do justice to You.
Please continue to change me,
So glimpses of heaven are revealed here and now.
Thank You for meeting my needs—
mental, physical, emotional, and spiritual—every day.
Help me experience Your love and forgiveness more and more,
So I have a model to love and forgive others.
Make clear the right thing to do,
So I can walk in the light and enjoy fellowship with You. Amen"

After that prayer he felt much calmer. One thing he knew for sure, if God was in this as he, and so many others believed, then nothing could thwart His plans. At that, he decided not to do anything except talk with Dennis and wait on the Lord.

He told Abigail about the phone call, his thought about Victoria, and the bind he felt he was in.

Chapter 26 – A Good Deed?

Abigail set down her orange juice. "So, what's the worst-case scenario?"

John sighed, rubbing his hands together. "If we can't prove the original sale was legitimate, we could lose the land."

Abigail nodded slowly. "And the best case?"

"Thomas finds some old records, some legal document that proves we're in the clear," he said with some resignation in his voice.

Abigail leaned forward. "John, God's fingerprints are all over this. Do you really think He brought us this far to let it fall apart now?"

John felt something inside him settle. "No," he said quietly. "I don't."

"When are you going to tell Dennis," she inquired.

"I'm heading over to the church as soon as we're finished with breakfast," he replied.

They had intended to spend the morning together, but she understood this needed to take precedence. "You go; I'll take care of the dishes," she told him.

***

It was just before 8:30 a.m. when he arrived at the church. Dennis was in his office, having just finished a team meeting. John walked in and closed the door behind him, so Dennis knew this was going to be a serious conversation.

"John, this must be more than just a building update. What's going on?" he asked with some concern in his voice.

John proceeded to share what Thomas had relayed and his concern about Victoria. He didn't go into detail about his conversation with her at the coffee shop, but he let Dennis know that it was an emotional conversation.

Dennis leaned back in his chair, rubbing his chin. "You're handling this better than I expected, John."

John exhaled slowly. "I had a moment earlier. But I prayed, and I know God is in this."

"That's strong faith," Dennis said, studying him. "Most people would be panicking."

John replied, "I don't know about that. I keep thinking about what Abigail said this morning—God brought us this far; He won't abandon us now."

Dennis nodded, then frowned. "Do you really think Victoria's behind this?"

He told Dennis, "I believe God is orchestrating something in Victoria's life. The last thing I want to do is jeopardize that by leveling a potentially false accusation at her."

From all his years pastoring and counseling, Dennis was a good listener and never interrupted as John unburdened himself. When John was finished, Dennis gave a slight smile. "John, you may not see it, but you have the heart of a pastor. The way you've handled this—with restraint and grace—it speaks volumes. And your concern for Victoria is admirable. Most people would have immediately confronted her. To be truthful, that would have been my first instinct too. I'm glad you waited. What do you see as our next steps?"

To hear that from a man he looked up to as a spiritual mentor meant a lot to John. "I appreciate the compliment, Dennis. I don't consider myself in the realm of a pastor. I prayed about this, and I think we should take our hands off of the steering wheel so to speak and let the Lord drive."

Dennis was surprised at John's response because he knew decisions still needed to be made about how they should proceed. "Do I take it that you want to keep moving ahead with the construction as is?"

"Yes," John confidently said. "We believe God is in this, so I don't see the need for this to go beyond us and Thomas. Let's keep moving ahead. He smiled slightly, recalling an old adage from his business days, 'Sometimes it's easier to ask for forgiveness than permission.' If a court order tells us to stop, then we'll comply, but short of that, let's keep doing what we're doing. Anything else might cause unnecessary worry and could hurt our ability to get donors and volunteers."

Dennis paused for a few moments then said, "I trust your instincts on this, John. Keep plowing ahead. As soon as you get new information, will you shoot me a text or give me a call?"

John agreed, and with that, the meeting ended as quickly as it had started. Here was yet another time when his faith would be tested. This was completely out of his hands, so he needed to wait on the Lord.

> **Reflection:** When our plans are interrupted, our instinct is to take control, to act, to fix. Too many people believe "If it's got to be then it's up to me" more than they do in the sovereignty of God. But often, the invitation is to wait, to rest in the knowledge that God is in control—just as Jesus was in the storm on the boat with the disciples. John's choice to step back and trust God rather than act in fear reflects true spiritual maturity. His prayer, grounded in surrender, shows us the real work of faith: not avoiding trials, but meeting them with courage, trust, and a willingness to let God lead. Where in your life might God be calling you to wait on Him, even when uncertainty clouds the path?

Chapter 27 – Don't be Anxious

"Be anxious for nothing, but in everything by prayer and supplication with thanksgiving let your requests be made known to God."

—Philippians 4:6

John was concerned about the deed situation, but he refused to let that concern give way to anxiety. He'd learned long ago to lean into the Apostle Paul's advice to the Philippians not to be anxious, but rather to lift up any and all concerns in prayer with thanksgiving. There were many times at MediTech when after doing all he could to make something work, he had to let go. It was never easy, but he realized it got easier with the passage of time.

He was thankful for the journey he'd been on since that first day when he heard Dennis share his vision for the community center. God's hand in everything was undeniable to a person of faith. He'd prayed and knew the circumstances were in God's hands. For his part, John tried his best to keep his eyes and ears open to see how God was working and might continue to use him and others.

A week passed and there were no updates from Thomas. John knew from his days running MediTech that the legal process can be excruciatingly slow sometimes. He advised Dennis they should keep moving forward to avoid stirring unnecessary concern—and that's exactly what he was doing.

***

Chapter 27 – Don't be Anxious

As was becoming his custom, he had a Monday morning meeting with Martha so she could update him on the construction progress.

This week they met at the church. When he walked in, he could see Martha busily typing on her phone. He made his way to her and said in his typical upbeat tone, "Good morning, Martha."

"Hi John," she replied without looking up. "Give me just a second to finish this text."

He pulled out his chair, sat down and spent a few moments taking in the hustle and bustle of people entering and exiting the church while Martha finished up. His mind briefly wandered back to all the times he spent with Duane, his longtime coach and friend from MediTech, at the coffee shop in Dallas as he learned the business. Those early years in his career were exciting times because everything felt so new. Now that he was older, newness had worn off, but he was excited because of the new purpose he'd found. Unlike a career, which can be very rewarding, the difference now was that his purpose felt eternal.

"Sorry about that, John," Martha said as she put her phone down. "Things are going well, and your tips around social proof and authority have been helpful but sometimes working with Bob feels like I'm dealing with my teenage boys," she said in an exasperated tone.

"Why do you say that?" John asked.

"Like my boys, we have a good relationship and he's not unsure what to do, but sometimes getting him to follow through is like pulling teeth," she told him.

John replied, "Give me an example."

She shared, "Bob has some proposed changes. They're small but we need to run them by the zoning board to be safe. I told him to get me the changes in writing last Wednesday and I still don't have them."

"Not to worry," John said. "Today I'll give you a couple of principles that can help to motivate people to take action." At that, Martha was all ears.

He went on, "There's a principle called consistency that nearly everyone responds to. In a nutshell, we feel better about ourselves when we keep our word. Have you ever given your word to someone but had to back out?" he inquired.

"Sure. Sometimes more important things pop up. I was going to do a girls weekend a few years ago but my husband got sick, so I stayed home with him," she shared.

"And how did you feel when you told your friends you couldn't make it?" he asked.

"They understood but I felt terrible because we'd spent months planning it," Martha replied.

"That was consistency at work on you. We feel better about ourselves, and look better to those we committed to, so we work extra hard to live up to our word. It's like Jesus said, 'Let your yes be yes and no be no' (Matthew 5:37), but it's working on others in this case. Now I'll give you the key." He paused to make sure she was paying close attention.

"Well, don't leave me hanging!" she said.

"Stop telling and start asking," he told her. "When you told Bob what you needed, he didn't commit so it's not likely he feels like he let you down. Simply asking and waiting for a response will help you immensely because Bob won't feel too good about himself if he fails to live up to his promise."

"It sounds so simple but what if he says he can't get me what I need in my timeframe?" she asked.

"Just because you needed the information by Monday didn't mean you needed to ask for it by Monday. If you'd have asked for it by the end of the day Thursday, he might have said yes. If he said no, you could fall back to Friday, then Monday. Remember what I shared about reciprocity?" he asked.

"Yes, but what's that got to do with reciprocity?"

John went on, "When you give a little by conceding, quite often people respond by conceding a little in return. This approach was incredibly helpful throughout my career. It was extremely rare that I didn't get what I wanted in the timeframe I needed it."

"Okay, I'll start trying that approach. What else do you have that can help me motivate Bob?" Martha asked.

"The other principle that motivates action is scarcity. When someone thinks they'll lose an opportunity or miss out on something, they tend to act rather quickly. If we don't gain something we may not feel worse off but if we think we're losing that same thing, we don't like how that feels, so we take action to avoid the loss." Again, John paused because he could see Martha was thinking.

"I think I get it, but an example would help," she replied.

"We both know Bob has a timeframe to get this project done. Not meeting that timeline could have lots of downsides for KDL. For example, some of his subcontractors might be slated for other jobs right after this one. What if he loses some of them before we finish? He might have to hire others and that could drive up costs and cut into KDL's profit," John told her.

"That makes sense. I could tell him that not getting his report on the proposed changes could set us back a week or more because we'd have to hold up on some aspects of the construction until the zoning board approves his modifications."

"That's a great approach. You're not trying to scare him, but you want to honestly alert him to what's at stake and how it might negatively impact him and KDL."

"John, while this is fresh on my mind, would you be okay if I called him right now?" she asked.

"Go for it," John said as he sipped his coffee.

Martha dialed Bob and he picked up right away. After a few pleasantries Martha said, "Bob, I know you have proposed changes. I really need those in writing ASAP because, depending on the timeliness and decision from the zoning board, it could cause some delays. We're both on a tight timeline and I know going over can mean big headaches for you."

"You're right about that," Bob interjected.

"Is there any chance you can get me the changes before the end of the day?" she asked then paused.

"I can't do that Martha because I'm already at the site and that will take at least an hour," he told her.

"I get it. Would you be able to write them up tonight, so I have them first thing in the morning," she asked as a fallback.

Bob paused to think, then replied, "I suppose I could get to it right after I leave the site this afternoon."

A smile broke out on Martha's face. "Thanks so much for agreeing to this Bob. It's going to be very helpful for both of us. For my part, the moment I hear back from the zoning board, I'll call you."

"I'd really appreciate that because I want to get going on the changes," Bob said as they hung up.

John sat back, smiling at the exchange. Moments like this reminded him why he loved coaching—watching others grow and succeed was a reward in itself. "Well?" John asked, grinning.

"That actually worked," she said, shaking her head. "I mean, I didn't have to nag him. I just asked the right way, and he agreed."

"Amazing what happens when people feel a sense of personal commitment," John told her.

Martha tapped her fingers against the table. "You know, I used to think influence was just about being pushy or convincing people. But this ... this is different. It's almost like," she paused, searching for the right words.

"Like guiding instead of pushing?" John offered.

"Exactly," she said. "I think I'm starting to get it."

Feeling a sense of accomplishment, John just sat back and smiled.

Martha looked at him and said, "It's easy to see how you helped turn MediTech into such a powerhouse. And I want to say with all humility, Dennis was right when he tapped you to lead this project."

"Thank you, Martha. That means a lot. We had an awkward start but just look at us now. I'm excited about seeing this through together."

With new momentum and shared purpose, they gathered their things and headed out—ready for whatever the next week might bring.

Reflection: True influence, like true leadership, is not about control but connection. As John and Martha learned, guiding others with humility and respect—through questions rather than commands, encouragement rather than pressure—reflects

God's own way of leading us. Jesus didn't coerce His followers; He invited them into relationship, asked them lots of questions, and walked with them in truth and love. John's mentorship of Martha is a small echo of this divine model. As we face our own "Bob moments"—frustrations, delays, unmet expectations—God invites us to step back from anxiety, lean into prayer, and trust that His Spirit is already at work in the hearts of those around us.

Chapter 28 – Three Days of Doubt

"But we were hoping that it was He who was going to redeem Israel. Indeed, besides all this, it is the third day since these things happened."

—Luke 24:21

Weeks passed, and construction pressed on—even though there was still no definitive word from Thomas about the deed. The more time passed, the more John and Dennis struggled to keep worry at bay and trust in God. During his career, John always felt he had some measure of control to influence outcomes, but this time was different. He decided to call Thomas to check on the status of the city's research into the issue with the deed.

"Thomas, it's been a while. I have to admit, I'm getting a bit anxious, so I thought I'd give you a call to find out how things are progressing," John asked.

"I wish I had more to tell you, John, but unfortunately there's no change. We're doing all we can as we comb through the archives. I know the family's attorney has asked to set a court date. They're understandably anxious to resolve this," he told John.

John's heart sank at that news. There was no way they'd end up in court without people finding out. Even if The Rock won, the mere fact of going to court could rattle everyone involved—and shake the confidence of supporters. "How likely is that, Thomas?"

"I learned this morning that the proposed court date is late afternoon this Friday. That gives us only three days. If we find the original deed and

Chapter 28 – Three Days of Doubt

get it to the judge before then, she might resolve it without the publicity of meeting in court," Thomas said with some resignation in his voice.

John replied, "Thanks, Thomas. I appreciate the work you've put into this and your candor. I'll relay everything to Dennis, and we'll continue to pray that you find the necessary paperwork." At that, they ended the call.

Still seated in his office, staring out the window, John thought of the desperate father who pleaded with Jesus to heal his son from the spirit that would come upon him, causing him to convulse and foam at the mouth. That loving father pleaded, "Lord, I believe; help my unbelief!" John could relate because he knew he was wavering between belief and unbelief. "Lord, help me," was all he said.

He walked out of his office and sat down in the kitchen where Abigail was busy putting away groceries. He began to fill her in on his conversation with Thomas and his struggling faith.

"Only three days until a possible court date?" she inquired.

"Yes, and to be honest, I feel defeated, like I'm losing hope," he said. That was a rare feeling for him and Abigail could clearly see it in his countenance.

"John, just because you don't see God's hand moving right now doesn't mean He isn't setting something in place," she said, hoping to bring him back to reality.

"I know you're right, but …" his voice trailed off.

"Think about how you've seen God at work when everyone around you missed it. No one knew God was at work when Joshua handed you that Gideon Bible," she reminded him.

He knew she was right but wondered why truth like that didn't settle him more.

"John, three days caught my attention. In a small way, you're just like the apostles. They had lost all hope when Christ was crucified but three days later their faith was renewed," she told him with some excitement in her voice.

John had not paused to think about anything except what was in the forefront of his mind—all the downside if they had to go to court, and especially if they lost. Jesus told his disciples everything that would transpire in advance regarding His death and resurrection but none of them were focused on that when He was crucified. Much like the disciples, John had lost sight of the fact that God had been divinely orchestrating so many things with the community center project. He thanked Abigail for her encouragement. While it did pick him up a bit, it was still difficult to let go of the concern he was feeling. It's often the case, even when others see God's hand at work, when the stakes are personal, faith often becomes a fight—between head knowledge and heart trust.

***

John drove to the church to speak with Dennis. While he could have called, he wanted to be in the presence of his pastor because he needed all the encouragement he could get. He wondered, "Was I wrong to not share the situation regarding the deed with everyone associated with the project? Will they feel deceived if everything falls through?" He wasn't concerned about his reputation; it was about people's faith being impacted like his was at this moment.

He ran into Dennis in the hallway and immediately Dennis saw a difference in John's countenance. "John, what's wrong? You don't look like your normal self."

"Dennis, I'm having a crisis of faith. Can we go somewhere private to talk?" John asked.

"Sure, let's go to my office," Dennis suggested. When they walked in, this time it was Dennis who closed the door.

John proceeded to share what Thomas had told him and his conversation with Abigail. "Dennis, I feel a sense of emptiness right now. It's an unfamiliar feeling and I don't know what to do about it," he confessed.

Dennis encouraged him, "What you're feeling is not unusual, John. I'm sure the disciples felt similar. I've no doubt that Abraham felt the same as he made his way to the altar with Isaac, his only son. All we can do at this point is trust and pray. God is bigger than our circumstances.

Chapter 28 – Three Days of Doubt

I choose to believe He is doing things we cannot see at this time. This isn't just about a court case or a deed. Maybe God is using this moment to teach you something deeper about surrender."

His words relieved John somewhat but John couldn't fully shake what he was feeling so the two decided to pray together. They bowed their heads and Dennis said, "Lord, you are the creator of heaven and earth. Nothing is outside of Your control, so we lift up this situation with the deed and court. No matter how things turn out, we know You have a plan, and no one can thwart it. Your word tells us, where two or more are gathered in Your name, you are there in their midst. Give us hope, renew our faith, and tangibly show us Your mighty hand in all of this. We pray this in the name of Jesus, Amen."

At that, John hugged Dennis, thanked him, and went home. As agonizing as it was, he made the decision to not do anything more until Friday. This was difficult for the man who was used to influencing the situations he found himself in. But this time, he realized there was nothing he could do except trust God's influence.

***

Thursday came and no word. John found himself checking his phone more than usual. He tried all he could to distract himself but to no avail. That evening he sat on the back patio, staring at the stars. He'd not done that in a while and was surprised at how bright they were. The thought hit him, "These are the same stars the Israelites would have seen during their wandering years in the desert, that David would have looked upon during his nights tending his flock, and that Abraham observed as he wondered about God fulfilling his promise to make a great nation out of his descendants." John understood he was no different than anyone who came before him. He knew God, but God was much bigger and mysterious than he realized.

Reflection: Faith doesn't eliminate doubt—it gives us a way through it. Like the disciples, John found himself in a place of confusion and waiting, unaware of what God might be doing behind the scenes. Trust often means releasing control and waiting—not passively, but prayerfully—with expectation. Under the same stars that guided the Israelites, Abraham, and David, John was reminded: God is always at work, just as Jesus said, even when we can't see it.

Chapter 29 – A Surprising Ally

"Then he (the Roman commander) called two of his centurions and ordered them, 'Get ready a detachment of two hundred soldiers, seventy horsemen, and two hundred spearmen to go to Caesarea at nine tonight. Provide horses for Paul so that he may be taken safely to Governor Felix.'"

—Acts 23:23–24

John woke up earlier than usual on Friday morning. Despite all his prayer, and the prayers of Dennis and Abigail, he was restless and couldn't sleep. He knew in his deepest being that he had little hope of things being resolved with the deed. He made his way downstairs to his office. He turned on the light and looked out the window into the darkness of the night.

"Lord, nothing is hidden from You. Just as you knew David, You've known me since the foundation of the world. You're outside time and space, so you know the beginning and the end of all things. You know how everything will unfold today. Please give me the peace that surpasses all understanding. Amen."

After that, he just stared out the window, trying to relax. Before he knew it, light began to fill the sky and nighttime yielded to daylight. He suddenly realized all his worry was gone. God had answered his prayer. No matter what happened next, he would be okay.

Another hour passed. He was a little startled when his phone rang, breaking the silence of the morning. "Hello," he said, not looking at the number or caller I.D.

It was Thomas. "John, I've got good news!" he said, barely able to contain himself.

John's heart leapt and he said with excitement, "Don't keep me in suspense. What is it?"

"We've resolved the issue. We have the original paperwork. Our attorney reviewed it and believes the sale was legitimate. He's on his way to the courthouse right now so he can give the paperwork to the judge as soon as she arrives."

John was practically in tears. His body felt limp as he silently gave thanks to the Lord. "Thomas, you'll never know how much this means to me!" he exclaimed. It wasn't just about the approval; it was about his faith.

What Thomas said next stunned John.

"Don't thank me, thank Victoria," Thomas said.

John didn't know how to respond. The only thing that came out of his voice was, "What?!" a mixture of bewilderment and excitement.

"You heard me right, John. Victoria is the one who located the paperwork. I had no idea she was researching this so I'm just as shocked as you. She gave the paperwork to me late last night. I didn't want to call you in the middle of the night because I wanted the attorney to review it first thing this morning."

"Do you need me to do anything, Thomas?" John asked.

Thomas replied, "No, just sit tight. As soon as the attorney lets me know how things went with the judge, I'll call you."

Within the hour Thomas called John to let him know everything was good. John sat in silence, still stunned at the news that Victoria, of all people, was the instrument God used to resolve the matter.

By now Abigail was up. She was in the bedroom making the bed when John entered. She knew something was up, so she said, "Well?"

John replied, "That's exactly what I said to Thomas."

"Don't leave me hanging," she said. "What did Thomas say?"

"They located the original files, everything is good!" he exclaimed.

She dropped the pillow that was in her hands, threw her arms around him and said, "Praise God! I'm so happy for you, John!"

Chapter 29 – A Surprising Ally

"That's not the biggest part of the news," he told her. After a short pause, he let her know, "It wasn't Thomas who located the information … it was Victoria!"

Abigail was almost as shocked as John at that news. She quickly sat on the bed and all she could say was, "What?!"

John laughed, "Again, that's exactly what I said to Thomas."

Despite several attempts, John had not heard from Victoria since their last meeting at the coffee shop. Given that she didn't show up for the groundbreaking ceremony, he assumed she was still adamantly opposed to the community center and that their last conversation had only strengthened her resolve to do whatever she could to stop the project. He felt bad for thinking that but truthfully, anyone would have harbored the same concern. He decided to give her another try so he could thank her.

After a few rings, Victoria picked up. "Hi John, how can I help you?" she asked in her familiar tone.

He replied, "You can't because you just did. I spoke to Thomas earlier and he told me you were the one who found the original deed and transaction papers. He said the community center can go ahead as planned. Thank you!"

"You're welcome," she replied, not betraying any emotion.

"I have to ask, why?" he said with sincere curiosity.

Victoria paused to collect her thoughts. "John, you were right about what you shared at the coffee shop. My pride wouldn't let me admit it at the time but as I thought about it over the ensuing weeks, you were correct. The anger I felt towards my father, God, the church, and truthfully, towards you, fueled my opposition to the community center despite knowing in my heart that it would be good for the children in our community. I'm starting to deal with all of that and felt the best way I could say I was sorry would be to use my resources and influence to help you. I'm truly sorry for the anxiety I've caused you."

John was speechless for a moment. "Victoria, you have no idea how much this means to so many people. But more than that, how much it means to me personally. I'm not just talking about the community center. I had no idea what would transpire the last time we were together. I felt bad about how things ended and that I'd not heard from you."

She knew John well enough by now to trust his sincerity. "I appreciate that, John. Please reach out if you need any further help on the community center."

"I'll certainly do that. It's always good to have friends in positions of authority. And the same goes for you. If you think I can help with issues that come up with the city, I'd be glad to return the favor."

When they hung up, both felt a great sense of satisfaction. For John, it was greater than he'd ever felt during his career. He was elated at the work God was doing in Victoria and her acknowledgement of it. For her part, Victoria was starting to experience a sense of freedom she'd not felt since she was a child. She no longer felt she always needed to be victorious and began to focus more energy on ways to collaborate with people for the betterment of Clairemont.

> **Reflection:** Just as he did with the Roman commander, God often works through the most unexpected people to accomplish His plans. Victoria, once an outspoken opponent, became the ally John never anticipated. This chapter reminds us that no one is beyond redemption and that seeds of grace, even when planted in difficult soil, can yield surprising fruit. When we release control and trust God's timing, He not only meets our needs—He often exceeds them in ways that deepen our faith and renew our awe of Him.

Chapter 30 – The Prodigal Returns

"But while he was still a long way off, his father saw him and felt compassion for him, and ran and embraced him and kissed him."

—Luke 15:20

True to her word, Victoria began to help with the community center. No project as big as that gets done without hiccups along the way. Whenever they arose, John leaned on her and Thomas to smooth things out. To Martha's delight, she and Bob finished the construction slightly ahead of schedule—a big win for both.

The community center officially opened almost six months after ground was broken on the construction. It was late Saturday morning when The Rock kicked off a huge celebration that featured a couple of local bands, food trucks, and games for the kids. Music and the smell of barbecue filled the air along with the laughter of children.

After lunch, Dennis stepped up to address the crowd. Thomas, Stan, Domonic, Joe, Sam, and most of the donors were in attendance. Dave and Beth were there as well. It caught John's eye that they were holding hands, which brought a smile to his face. He'd still not heard from Dave, but he was satisfied knowing God was at work restoring their marriage.

Dennis began, "Nearly a year ago I shared a vision with the congregation of The Rock. It was that we'd have a safe space for our children to enjoy, a place where they could grow and learn. It's one thing to have a vision but quite another to make it a reality. We could not have done it without our congregation's generosity along with the generosity of so many individuals and businesses here in Clairemont and the surrounding area. Thank you to all of you who have expressed an interest in volunteering. That's when the real work begins. Most of all, I want to express my deepest thanks to John Andrews."

At that, John blushed, and Abigail squeezed his hand. Dennis went on, "John's influence and faith are the cornerstone of this building. I don't think it would have come about without him. And just as important as that, as his pastor it's been a joy to see his faith grow by leaps and bounds through the entire process. John, please come up and say a few words."

John wasn't expecting this and had not prepared anything to share. Nonetheless, he made his way to Dennis who handed him the mic.

Pausing to gather himself, John said, "Thank you, Dennis, not only for your kind words but for trusting me with the opportunity to shepherd this project. When I left my corporate career, I began to feel a void and needed as sense of purpose. Little did I realize it would come as it did. I thought purpose meant success. Then one afternoon, I met a man handing out Gideon Bibles in a parking lot, and everything changed. In addition to that blessing, it's been a joy to work with all of you."

He paused again, this time to look at Dennis, Dave, Thomas, Martha, and several others. It was his special way of acknowledging each and they felt it.

He went on, "The community center isn't just a building, and it won't be limited to the activities our children enjoy. I believe it will have an eternal impact for many people."

At that, he looked directly at Victoria. She smiled and John could see her eyes were getting moist. "For my part, for the first time, God became alive and intimately involved in my life. I experienced so many things that were unmistakably His divine intervention. And let me say emphatically, I'm no different than any of you. He wants to be involved in your lives too. I will simply end with this; God, please open everyone's eyes and ears, that they might see and hear You as I have this past year and experience all the joy that comes with knowing You."

As he handed the microphone back to Dennis, a spontaneous cheer broke out. He hugged Abigail and they shed more than a few tears of joy.

Chapter 30 – The Prodigal Returns

People enjoyed themselves as the rest of the day unfolded. Many grateful people made their way to John. For his part, he made it a point to thank each person who helped him and every donor he could find in the growing crowd. Although he could only spend a few minutes with each, he had a way about him that made everyone feel that they were the only person who mattered.

***

The next day John and Abigail attended the Sunday morning service. Dennis addressed the congregation and talked about the community center in more vivid detail. He didn't want the Saturday celebration to be overtly religious, but he threw caution to the wind with his church family. He and John shared vivid stories of God's providence at work and talked about how they felt they were living a biblical story, just like the people in the Bible.

As one would expect, the church was packed that day, standing room only. As John spoke, he glanced around the sanctuary. He couldn't explain why, but something felt different. Then, in the back row near the exit, he saw her—a new face in the sea of people. Victoria was seated in the last row in an aisle seat. The prodigal had come home. When he saw her, he smiled because he knew, just as had been the case for him, she'd been *Influenced from Above*.

> **Reflection:** In a world in which influence is often wielded for personal gain, John's journey shows us a higher calling—to influence with humility, grace, and trust in God's timing. Each step, from marketplace wisdom to spiritual awakening, reveals how true transformation happens not through control, but through connection—first with people, then with the divine. The culmination of the community center is more than a physical structure; it's a testament to lives changed, relationships redeemed, and faith made tangible. Like John, we're invited to see

our own influence as part of something eternal—an opportunity to sow good, love well, and be vessels through which others are *Influenced from Above*.

A Deeper Exploration of the Faith–Influence Connection

"But he said to him, 'If they do not listen to Moses and the Prophets, they will not be persuaded even if someone rises from the dead.'"

—Luke 16:31

I hope you enjoyed *Influenced from Above* and John's spiritual journey as he connected the dots between faith and influence in a deeply personal and practical way. The ability to influence and persuade others has been a part of the human experience since the beginning of time. Every day, each of us communicates with people hoping to influence how they think, feel, or behave—for a variety of reasons, personal and professional.

Here's a hard truth; not everyone can be persuaded, even by the most persuasive people who ever lived. Although He is divine, always spoke the truth in love, performed miracles, and rose from the dead, Jesus did not persuade everyone to believe in Him. Even the Apostle Paul—with his great intellect and profound impact on the early church and Western culture—couldn't persuade everyone to believe.

I recall a conversation, decades ago, at an Ahearn family reunion when I spoke with a cousin. He was adamantly opposed to faith and had no problem sharing that fact. The more we spoke, the angrier he seemed to get. I realized nothing I could say or do would change his position. Then I heard this come out of my mouth, "I used to think if Jud (our Bible study leader) or Rich (our pastor) were here, they'd explain it better. But now I understand—Jesus was here, and they killed Him. It doesn't matter what you think, I know what I'm sharing with you is the truth."

My goal in writing this book is to help you see the connection between faith and influence. I want you to feel good about your attempts to influence people ethically and I hope you'll grow in your ability to do so. To encourage your growth, I've included a concise recap of key concepts from the book.

Below are the principles of influence popularized by Robert Cialdini, PhD. Cialdini is a Regents Professor Emeritus at Arizona State University, where he taught for more than 30 years. He is the most cited living social psychologist in the world when it comes to the science of ethical influence. I had the privilege of learning about influence directly from him. I've known Cialdini for more than 20 years as of the writing of this book. The highest praise I can share with you is this—his work profoundly changed the course of both my career and life.

For each principle I've shared seven scriptures and give you connection points for each. The list of scriptures is by no means exhaustive. I've no doubt there are hundreds of passages that could apply to each principle, so why seven? One story in particular comes to mind. Elijah's servant had to return to the sea seven times before he finally saw what Elijah wanted him to see (1 Kings 18:43-44). I hope these seven scriptures per principle will help you see the faith-influence connection.

1. Liking

The principle of liking highlights a reality we all intuitively understand; we're more likely to say "yes" to people we know, like, and trust. When someone is a friend, it's easy to say "yes" to them.

The key to this principle is to approach people with the following mindset—I want to like the people I'm with. I encourage you to take it upon yourself to find ways to like the people you interact with. Two simple things you can do to make this happen are finding out what you have in common and offering sincere compliments.

Proverbs 17:17 – "A friend loves at all times, and a brother is born for adversity."

Connection: True friendships are built on love and support during good and bad times, creating deep bonds that naturally foster trust and cooperation.

Proverbs 27:9 – "Oil and perfume make the heart glad, so a man's counsel is sweet to his friend."

Connection: Genuine, heartfelt advice from a friend strengthens trust and deepens relational bonds.

John 13:35 – "By this all men will know that you are My disciples, if you have love for one another."

Connection: Friendship isn't necessarily love, but it can grow into it. Love and care within a community serve as a powerful testimony that attracts others and fosters mutual trust.

Romans 12:10 – "Be devoted to one another in brotherly love; give preference to one another in honor."

Connection: It's easy to put a friend's wellbeing and needs above your own.

1 Peter 4:8 – "Above all, keep fervent in your love for one another, because love covers a multitude of sins."

Connection: Deep love fosters forgiveness and understanding, allowing relationships to flourish even through the most challenging times.

Proverbs 18:24 – "A man of too many friends comes to ruin, but there is a friend who sticks closer than a brother."

Connection: Genuine friendship goes beyond surface-level interactions, creating loyalty and trust that endure over time.

James 2:8 – "If, however, you are fulfilling the royal law according to the Scripture, 'You shall love your neighbor as yourself,' you are doing well."

Connection: Showing love and respect towards others establishes trust and goodwill, key components of influence and relationship building.

2. Unity

Unity emphasizes shared identity and belonging. It's easier for us to say "yes" to people we feel a deep bond with, those with whom we have a shared identity. That's so because it's almost as if we're saying "yes" to ourselves. I often tell audiences, "It's not about cheering for the same team; it's playing for the same team."

Ephesians 5:29 tells us, "For no one ever hated his own flesh, but nourishes and cherishes it, just as Christ also does the church." When we experience unity, we love others more easily because it's almost like loving ourselves.

Psalm 133:1 – "Behold, how good and how pleasant it is for brothers to dwell together in unity!"

Connection: Unity creates harmony and a sense of shared purpose, fostering a cooperative spirit.

John 17:21 – "That they may all be one; even as You, Father, are in Me and I in You, that they also may be in Us, so that the world may believe that You sent Me."

Connection: Shared identity in Christ fosters unity and collective purpose because unity creates brothers and sisters.

Ephesians 4:3 – "Being diligent to preserve the unity of the Spirit in the bond of peace."

Connection: Unity requires intentional effort and serves as a foundation for peace and collaboration.

Romans 12:5 – "So we, who are many, are one body in Christ, and individually members one of another."

Connection: Shared identity as part of one body fosters mutual dependence and cooperation. Again, "No one has ever hated his own body" (Ephesians 5:29).

Galatians 3:28 – "There is neither Jew nor Greek, there is neither slave nor free man, there is neither male nor female; for you are all one in Christ Jesus."

Connection: Unity transcends social and cultural boundaries, creating a sense of belonging.

Philippians 2:2 – "Make my joy complete by being of the same mind, maintaining the same love, united in spirit, intent on one purpose."

Connection: Shared love and purpose create an environment of mutual trust and harmony.

Romans 15:5–6 – "Now may the God who gives perseverance and encouragement grant you to be of the same mind with one another according to Christ Jesus, so that with one accord you may with one voice glorify the God and Father of our Lord Jesus Christ."

Connection: Unity in mindset creates a strong foundation for collaboration and mutual support.

3. Reciprocity

Reciprocity is the obligation we naturally feel to give back to people who first give to us. According to social psychologists, every human society teaches its people reciprocity because we learned long ago that it's easier to survive if we help one another.

When liking or unity are at play, our giving is received differently because it's more authentic. That's because we naturally want the best for friends, family, and other loved ones. This approach moves our giving from transactional to relational.

Luke 6:31 – "Treat others the same way you want them to treat you."

Connection: Treating others with kindness and respect builds mutual trust and rapport, making them more inclined to respond positively.

Luke 6:38 – "Give, and it will be given to you."

Connection: Generosity creates a virtuous cycle of reciprocity and builds mutual goodwill.

Proverbs 11:25 – "The generous man will be prosperous, and he who waters will himself be watered."

Connection: Helping others often leads to blessings and reciprocity. We don't give to get, but if we don't give, we shouldn't expect to get.

Galatians 6:7 – "Do not be deceived, God is not mocked; for whatever a man sows, this he will also reap."

Connection: Kindness given will often return in kind, in this life and the next. By the same token, unkind acts are likely to be reciprocated too, so beware!

2 Corinthians 9:6 – "He who sows sparingly will also reap sparingly, and he who sows bountifully will also reap bountifully."

Connection: Generosity leads to abundance and reciprocal blessings. Help enough others and they'll want to help you in return, which makes reaching your goals and dreams much easier.

Proverbs 19:17 – "One who is gracious to a poor man lends to the Lord, and He will repay him for his good deed."

Connection: Generosity towards others is ultimately reciprocated by God.

Acts 20:35 – "Remember the words of the Lord Jesus, that He Himself said, 'It is more blessed to give than to receive.'"

Connection: Giving creates blessings both for the giver and receiver. When you embrace this truth, you realize the amount of blessing you experience is unlimited because there are so many people you can help.

4. Authority

The principle of authority illustrates the reality that we more willingly follow the lead of trusted experts. When someone knows more than we do, following their lead usually saves us time, money, and energy.

A key here is to make sure people know about your expertise *before* you try to influence them. Sharing your sources of information also engages this principle. Never forget; two people can say the same thing, but it's the expert who's likely to be believed.

Romans 13:1 – "Every person is to be in subjection to the governing authorities. For there is no authority except from God, and those which exist are established by God."

Connection: This verse highlights that legitimate authority is ultimately established by God. Deferring to such authority brings order and aligns with divine wisdom.

Proverbs 1:7 – "The fear of the Lord is the beginning of knowledge; fools despise wisdom and instruction."

Connection: True wisdom begins with recognizing and respecting God's ultimate authority. Knowledge and credibility stem from honoring divine guidance.

Matthew 7:29 – "For He was teaching them as one having authority, and not as their scribes."

Connection: Jesus's authority was evident through His teaching, which inspired confidence and trust because it carried weight and authenticity.

Hebrews 13:17 – "Obey your leaders and submit to them, for they keep watch over your souls as those who will give an account."

Connection: Spiritual leaders are entrusted with guiding others under God's authority. Trusting their leadership creates order and spiritual well-being.

Titus 2:15 – "These things speak and exhort and reprove with all authority. Let no one disregard you."

Connection: Spiritual authority involves teaching and correction. Exercising it effectively builds trust and respect among followers.

Proverbs 8:15–16 – "By me kings reign, and rulers decree justice. By me princes rule, and nobles, all who judge rightly."

Connection: True authority operates under God's wisdom and justice. Recognizing this authority fosters trust and respect for leadership.

Acts 5:29 – "But Peter and the apostles answered, 'We must obey God rather than men.'"

Connection: When human authority conflicts with divine authority, allegiance to God takes precedence. This principle reinforces the ultimate source of credibility and moral leadership.

5. Social Proof

Humans are social creatures and as such, we follow the lead of others, especially when those people are similar to us. What other people think, feel, and do, has a huge impact on how we think, how we feel, and what we do.

The key to ethical influence when using social proof is to share what similar others are doing. If what's being shared or proposed works for people like us, then we naturally assume it will probably work for us as well.

Hebrews 12:1 – "Therefore, since we have so great a cloud of witnesses surrounding us, let us also lay aside every encumbrance and the sin which so easily entangles us, and let us run with endurance the race that is set before us."

Connection: The example of past faithful believers serves as social proof, encouraging us to remain steadfast in faith as they did.

Proverbs 13:20 – "He who walks with wise men will be wise, but the companion of fools will suffer harm."

Connection: Associating with the right people shapes character and decision making, reinforcing the power of group influence. We become like the people we surround ourselves with.

Philippians 3:17 – "Brethren, join in following my example, and observe those who walk according to the pattern you have in us."

Connection: Observing and imitating strong examples of faith, such as the Apostle Paul, encourages us to follow the same path and reap the spiritual rewards.

Acts 2:42 – "They were continually devoting themselves to the apostles' teaching and to fellowship, to the breaking of bread and to prayer."

Connection: The collective devotion of early Christians demonstrated the power of group behavior, attracting more people to the faith.

1 Thessalonians 1:6-7 – "You also became imitators of us and of the Lord, having received the word in much tribulation with the joy of the Holy Spirit, so that you became an example to all the believers in Macedonia and in Achaia."

Connection: The Thessalonians followed the example of early Christians, proving that seeing other's faithfulness reinforces one's own commitment.

Matthew 5:16 – "Let your light shine before men in such a way that they may see your good works and glorify your Father who is in heaven."

Connection: Visible acts of faith and righteousness from believers can be a form of social proof, inspiring others to glorify God.

John 13:15 – "For I gave you an example that you also should do as I did to you."

Connection: Jesus's actions serve as the ultimate social proof, guiding believers in how to love and serve others.

6. Consistency

We feel internal psychological pressure, and external social pressure, to be consistent in what we say and do. It boils down to word and deed. We feel better about ourselves when we keep our word, and we look better to those we committed to.

The key here is always to remember that when you're trying to influence people, consistency is about the other person. What have they said or done? What do they believe and value? If you can align your request with those insights, it becomes easier for them to say "yes."

Matthew 5:37 – "But let your statement be, 'Yes, yes' or 'No, no'; anything beyond these is of evil."

Connection: Jesus emphasizes the importance of integrity and reliability—keeping one's word strengthens trust and influence.

James 5:12 – "But above all, my brethren, do not swear, either by heaven or by earth or with any other oath; but your yes is to be yes, and your no, no, so that you may not fall under judgment."

Connection: Repeating the teaching of Jesus, James reinforces that unwavering honesty in commitments builds credibility. There's no need for showy acts like swearing on a stack of Bibles.

Psalm 15:4 – "In whose eyes a reprobate is despised, but who honors those who fear the Lord; He swears to his own hurt and does not change."

Connection: True commitment means standing by one's promises, even when inconvenient, proving reliability and trustworthiness.

2 Corinthians 1:20 – "For as many as are the promises of God, in Him they are yes; therefore, also through Him is our Amen to the glory of God through us."

Connection: God's unwavering faithfulness serves as the ultimate model for keeping commitments and being consistent.

Ecclesiastes 5:5 – "It is better that you should not vow than that you should vow and not pay."

Connection: This verse highlights the weight of commitments—better to refrain from making promises than to break them.

Luke 16:10 – "He who is faithful in a very little thing is faithful also in much; and he who is unrighteous in a very little thing is unrighteous also in much."

Connection: Consistency in small matters proves one's reliability and builds trust for greater responsibilities.

Psalm 119:106 – "I have sworn, and I will confirm it, that I will keep Your righteous ordinances."

Connection: Commitment to God's word and principles reflects unwavering faith and consistency in one's actions.

7. Scarcity

Scarcity tells us the very real human experience; we value things more when we learn they are rare or diminishing. This isn't about fearmongering or using scare tactics. It's about honestly alerting people to what they might lose by not taking action.

If you've tapped into liking or unity, then I trust that you want what's best for your friends and loved ones. That should spur you on to share why they might want to act sooner rather than later so they don't miss an opportunity.

Psalm 90:12 – "So teach us to number our days, that we may present to You a heart of wisdom."

Connection: Recognizing the limited nature of life encourages us to live wisely and make the most of our time.

Isaiah 55:6 – "Seek the Lord while He may be found; call upon Him while He is near."

Connection: God's invitation is available for a time, but delaying may mean missing the opportunity.

John 9:4 – "We must work the works of Him who sent Me as long as it is day; night is coming when no one can work."

Connection: Jesus reminds us that time is limited, and we must take advantage of the opportunities we have to do good.

Matthew 25:10-13 – "And while they were going away to make the purchase, the bridegroom came, and those who were ready went in with him to the wedding feast; and the door was shut. Later the other virgins also came, saying, 'Lord, lord, open up for us.' But he answered, 'Truly I say to you, I do not know you.' Be on the alert then, for you do not know the day nor the hour."

Connection: Readiness is crucial, as the door to opportunity may close when least expected.

James 4:14 – "Yet you do not know what your life will be like tomorrow. You are just a vapor that appears for a little while and then vanishes away."

Connection: Life is fleeting, emphasizing the need to take meaningful action while we can.

Hebrews 3:13 – "But encourage one another day after day, as long as it is still called 'Today,' so that none of you will be hardened by the deceitfulness of sin."

Connection: Today is the only time we are guaranteed, so we must seize opportunities while they exist.

Matthew 6:19-21 – "Do not store up for yourselves treasures on earth, where moth and rust destroy, and where thieves break in and steal. But store up for yourselves treasures in heaven, where neither moth nor rust destroys, and where thieves do not break in or steal; for where your treasure is, there your heart will be also."

Connection: Earthly wealth is temporary and fleeting, reinforcing the value of eternal investments.

Heart, Mind, Body, and Soul

The late Dallas Willard, philosophy professor at the University of Southern California and author of *The Divine Conspiracy* and *Renovation of the Heart*, shaped my thinking more than anyone else around the concepts of heart, soul, mind, and body.

The heart—also known as the spirit or will Biblically—isn't just an organ that pumps blood. It's the place where our deepest beliefs and desires reside, the source from which our character flows. Some of those beliefs and desires are so deeply embedded within us that we're not always fully aware of who we are or what we truly want. Ben Franklin rightly observed, "There are three things extremely hard: steel, a diamond, and to know one's self." Self-discovery is a lifelong journey in which God reveals who we are in relation to Him. That's one reason the author of Proverbs wrote, "The fear of the Lord is the beginning of knowledge"

(Proverbs 1:7). Above all else, Jesus tells us it's the heart—the inside of the cup—that must change, if we want true goodness to flow from within.

The mind—is where we think, both consciously and subconsciously. Did you know that science has shown that fewer than 5% of the decisions we make each day are conscious? God designed our brains to learn and then shift routine tasks to the background (the subconscious), allowing us to conserve mental energy for bigger, more demanding decisions. By definition, subconscious thoughts are below our conscious awareness, yet they drive the vast majority of our daily actions and decisions.

The body—represents what we do. Unlike God, our thoughts alone don't create reality. Our bodies are the vehicles through which we bring thoughts to life. In a very real sense, the body has "a mind of its own" because it remembers through feelings. We are pleasure seekers and pain avoiders by design, and because of that, feelings can drive actions long before conscious thought has a chance to intervene. Over time, these feelings shape habits, and many of those habits run on autopilot, making it difficult for us to change. The Apostle Paul describes this tension beautifully in Romans 8:14-25:

"For we know that the Law is spiritual, but I am of flesh, sold into bondage to sin. For what I am doing, I do not understand; for I am not practicing what I would like to do, but I am doing the very thing I hate. But if I do the very thing I do not want to do, I agree with the Law, confessing that the Law is good. So now, no longer am I the one doing it, but sin which dwells in me. For I know that nothing good dwells in me, that is, in my flesh; for the willing is present in me, but the doing of the good is not. For the good that I want, I do not do, but I practice the very evil that I do not want. But if I am doing the very thing I do not want, I am no longer the one doing it, but sin which dwells in me. I find then the principle that evil is present in me, the one who wants to do good. For I joyfully concur with the law of God in the inner man, but I see a different law in the members of my body, waging war against the law of my mind and making me a prisoner of the law of sin which is in my members. Wretched man that I am! Who will set me free from the body of this death? Thanks be to God through Jesus Christ our Lord! So then, on the one hand I myself with my mind am serving the law of God, but on the other, with my flesh the law of sin."

Our soul—brings together heart, mind, and body to present our unified self to the world. When our heart isn't renewed, our thoughts and desires remain misaligned with God, and we fall back into old bodily habits. In that state, the soul is in distress. But here's the good news: when our heart, mind, and body are rightly oriented toward God, our soul finds peace—the kind that surpasses all understanding (Philippians 4:7).

Dallas Willard's View on Soul, Heart, Mind, and Body

Human Dimension	Definition	Role	Transformation
Soul	Unifies the heart, mind, and body into a cohesive life.	Oversees the harmony and integration of all human dimensions.	Requires alignment with God for inner peace and spiritual wholeness.
Heart (Will/Spirit)	The executive center of the person; the seat of our intentions, desires, and decisions.	Directs actions and shapes character through choices.	Must be renewed by God to align with His will and purposes.
Mind	The center of both conscious and subconscious thought, shaping our perceptions and decisions.	Processes information, discerns truth, and guides action.	Needs renewal through reflection on God's truth and wisdom.
Body	The physical vessel through which we interact with the world.	Acts on the directives of the heart, mind, and feelings; executes intentions.	Must be retrained through spiritual disciplines to serve God faithfully.

Cialdini's Principles and Willard's Framework Alignment

Willard's Framework	Core Motives	Biblical Alignment	Cialdini's Principles
Heart	Building Relationships	Proverbs 27:19 – "As in water face reflects face, so the heart of man reflects man."	Liking, Reciprocity
Mind	Overcoming Uncertainty	Philippians 4:8 – "Finally, brethren, whatever is true, whatever is honorable, whatever is right, whatever is pure, whatever is lovely, whatever is of good repute, if there is any excellence and if anything worthy of praise, dwell on these things."	Authority, Social Proof
Body	Motivating Action	James 1:22 – "But prove yourselves doers of the word, and not merely hearers who delude themselves."	Consistency, Scarcity
Soul	Shared Identity	John 17:21 – "That they may all be one; even as You, Father, are in Me and I in You, that they also may be in Us, so that the world may believe that You sent Me."	Unity

The Ethics of Influence

Always remember, the principles of influence are neutral tools. A hammer can be used to drive nails and build a home, or it can be used to harm. The difference lies not in the tool, but in how it's wielded. Influence works the same way—it's how we use it that determines whether it's ethical and reveals our character. Aristotle put it well when he said, "Character may almost be called the most effective means of persuasion."

When attempting to influence people, three essential questions can help to ensure your approach is ethical—even from a purely secular standpoint.

1. Am I being truthful?

It's not enough simply to tell the truth—you also can't hide the truth. If there's information you know will materially impact someone's decision, you're obligated to disclose it early on. Here's the good news: when you proactively bring up a potential weakness or drawback in your request, you actually earn trust because people will view you as an honest individual.

2. Am I only using principles of influence that naturally present themselves?

What does this mean? Let's consider two common tactics manipulators use:

They claim, "everyone is doing this" (social proof) when it's not true. By inventing a crowd, they pressure people into compliance.

They create false scarcity, suggesting something is in short supply or time-limited to spur action—when it's not.

Ethical influencers only use principles of influence that are naturally present in the situation.

3. Is it wise for the other person to say "yes"?

Let's be honest: when you attempt to influence someone, there's usually something in it for you. But will a "yes" response also benefit them? As Stephen Covey wrote in *The 7 Habits of Highly Effective People*, aim for win-win outcomes. I simplify it this way: "Good for you, good for me, then we're good to go."

If you can say yes to all three questions, you can feel confident that your influence is both ethical and honorable.

What does the Bible say about ethical influence?
A lot! As John Andrews discovered, influence isn't just about professional success or personal happiness. While they are important, influence can also have eternal impact when used with the right motives.

Consider the Pharisees. They were more concerned with position and status than with truly serving people. They laid burdens on others they were unwilling to carry themselves (Matthew 23:1-12). They did good deeds to look good, focusing on outward appearance rather than inward transformation. Jesus rebuked them, pronouncing eight woes, and urged them to clean the inside of the cup—their hearts—so that good deeds would flow naturally (Matthew 23:13-36).

The Old Testament offers plenty of examples of manipulation too—Rachel prompting Jacob to deceive Isaac, Jacob's many schemes, and Delilah's manipulation of Samson. In each case, they didn't trust God to fulfill His promises in His timing. But here's the truth: God's plans will never be thwarted by Satan or humans.

Jesus urges us to trust God, to seek Him first with all our heart, and not to lean on our own understanding. We don't see the eternal picture—but He does. That's why Paul assures us, "God causes all things to work together for good to those who love God, to those who are called according to His purpose" (Romans 8:28). This might shock you, but the promise is not for everyone. Paul was clear—it's only for those who love God and respond to His call.

Ultimately, ethical influence begins with our motives, and they originate from the heart. Pure motives come from a heart that has been transformed by God. The prophet Ezekiel put it this way, "And I will give them one heart and put a new spirit within them. And I will take the heart of stone out of their flesh and give them a heart of flesh" (Ezekiel 11:19).

When God transforms our hearts, our influence becomes not just ethical—but also eternally significant.

> **Final Reflection:** The journey of *Influenced from Above* is about more than understanding principles of persuasion—it's about transformation. It's about realizing that every conversation, every act of leadership, and every attempt to influence others is ultimately an opportunity to reflect God's character in the world. Influence, when grounded in faith, becomes a sacred calling—a chance to bless, to build, and to lead others not by force, but through love and truth. As you continue your own journey, may you influence others ethically, powerfully, and with the confidence that God Himself is working through you—not just to change minds, but also to touch hearts, shape lives, and leave a legacy that echoes into eternity.

Characters in Order of Appearance

Main Characters

John Andrews (Protagonist, Former CEO, Church Leader)
- A former corporate executive of MediTech searching for purpose after retirement.
- Becomes the leader of The Rock's community center project, learning to integrate faith and ethical influence.
- Wrestles with balancing leadership, faith, and the ethical use of persuasion.

Abigail Andrews (John's Wife, Support System)
- John's loving and wise partner, offering emotional and spiritual support.
- Encourages John to pray and reflect when faced with challenges.
- Challenges John's thinking by pushing him to consider how faith and influence intersect.

Dennis Reacher (Senior Pastor of The Rock)
- A visionary pastor focused on community outreach and making faith practical.
- Invites John to lead the community center project, believing it is a divine appointment.
- Encourages John to trust in God's timing and guidance.

Dave Sargent (Church Elder, Retired Army Major, Businessman)
- A respected elder and John's closest ally in launching the community center project.
- Experiences a personal moral failure, which tests John's leadership and integrity.
- Ultimately steps away from leadership due to personal struggles.

Victoria Sparks (Clairemont City Council and School Board Member, Main Antagonist)
- A strong-willed political figure who opposes the community center due to its faith-based roots.
- Holds a deep-seated resentment toward religion stemming from childhood wounds.
- Slowly begins to question her stance as she interacts more with John.

Martha Cook (Retired IT Project Manager, Longtime Church Member)
- A dedicated but frustrated church member who initially feels overlooked.
- Opposes the project due to personal hurt and financial concerns but is won over after a heartfelt conversation with John.
- Becomes a key supporter once she recognizes her objections were more personal than practical.

Supporting Characters

Beth Sargent (Dave's Wife)
- Devoted wife and longtime church member.
- Initially unaware of Dave's moral failure but later confronts the reality of his choices.
- Her reaction deeply impacts both their marriage and the church community.

Joshua (Old Man Handing out Gideon Bibles)
- John meets Joshua while struggling with his purpose and wondering if God actually answers specific prayers.

Characters in Order of Appearance

- His encounter with John confirms God's leading and symbolizes a divine appointment.

Domonic Mancini (Owner of Mancini's Italian Restaurant)
- A friendly and well-liked restaurant owner who supports the project from the start.
- Indirectly endorses the project by excitedly discussing it with Thomas May before John's meeting.

Thomas May (Clairemont City Council Member)
- A pragmatic politician who is hesitant but open-minded about the community center project.
- Initially concerned about public backlash but gradually becomes an ally.
- His endorsement helps to sway other council members to approve the project.

Stan Letterman (Editor of the Clairemont Courier Newspaper)
- A fair and objective journalist interested in covering the community center project.
- Victoria tries to use him to publish negative press against the project.
- After speaking with John, he writes a balanced article, helping to sway public opinion in favor of the project.

Tim Rhodes (Zoning Board Member)
- A longtime Clairemont resident and key figure in the zoning approval process.
- Has no strong religious beliefs but respects The Rock's community impact.
- Despite Victoria's influence, he remains neutral and ultimately supports the project.

Samuel Levitt (Jewish Business Owner, Influential Community Figure)
- A respected business leader who initially supports the project.

- Becomes hesitant after Victoria sows doubt about religious involvement in the center.
- John persuades him using ethical influence, and he ultimately becomes a key supporter.

Kurt Miller (Business Owner)
- Owner of Ease of Business IT.
- Did business with MediTech when John was still CEO.
- Agrees to fund ongoing expenses for the community center based on his prior relationship with John.

Joe Walls (Church Member, Architect)
- Volunteers his expertise as an architect for the community center.
- Initially resistant to making compromises on zoning requests.
- Learns about ethical influence from John, helping him grow both professionally and personally.

Bob Holmes (Construction Lead)
- Site supervisor for KDL Construction working on the community center.
- Had early issues following through on concerns raised by Martha.
- A local resident with children who will benefit from the center.

Unnamed Characters

Various Church Members
- Many are excited about the community center, while others are concerned about finances and volunteering.
- Martha becomes their informal spokesperson before she changes her stance.

Various Business Owners
- Some are hesitant to get involved due to Victoria's influence and concerns over public perception.
- Others see the value in the project after John frames it as a true community effort.

City Council
- A mix of supporters and skeptics who need to approve the community center.
- Eventually, they approve the project despite Victoria's efforts to stop it.

Zoning Board Members
- A mix of supporters and skeptics who ensure the project meets city regulations.
- Ultimately, they approve the project with minor revisions.

About the Author

Brian Ahearn is the founder of Influence PEOPLE, LLC, and a faculty member at the prestigious Cialdini Institute. An international speaker, trainer, coach, and consultant, he helps clients to apply research-based approaches to influence to achieve greater professional success at work and personal happiness at home.

Brian was personally trained by Robert Cialdini, PhD, the most cited living social psychologist in the world on the science of ethical influence. He is one of only a dozen individuals currently to hold the coveted Cialdini Method Certified Trainer (CMCT®) designation and one of just a handful who have earned the Cialdini Pre-suasion Trainer (CPT®) designation.

His first book, *Influence PEOPLE: Powerful Everyday Opportunities to Persuade that are Lasting and Ethical*, was not only an Amazon bestseller, but was also named one of the Top 100 Influence Books of All Time by the Book Authority.

Brian's follow-up book, *Persuasive Selling for Relationship-Driven Insurance Agents*, was an Amazon new release bestseller in several categories.

His third book, *The Influencer: Secrets to Success and Happiness*, is a business parable that shows readers how ethical influence can lead to success at work and happiness at home.

Brian's most recent book, *His Story, My Story, Our Story*, explores his relationship with his late father, a Captain in the U.S. Marine Corps during the Vietnam War.

A LinkedIn Learning author, Brian's courses on applying influence in sales and coaching have been viewed by more than 800,000 learners worldwide. In addition, more than one million people have watched Brian's TEDx talk on pre-suasion.

When Brian isn't influencing people, he enjoys reading, traveling, working out, good Scotch and cigars, and spending time with his wife, Jane. Together, they have one daughter, Abigail, an American Sign Language interpreter and paraprofessional in local school systems. Abigail and her husband, Tyler, welcomed their first child, Emmett James Ahearn, in March 2025. Brian and Jane live in Westerville, Ohio.

Looking for a speaker for your next event?

Connect with Brian on LinkedIn:
https://www.linkedin.com/in/brianfahearn/

Visit Brian's website: https://www.influencepeople.biz

Email Brian: Brian.Ahearn@influencepeople.biz

www.ingramcontent.com/pod-product-compliance
Lightning Source LLC
Chambersburg PA
CBHW060600080526
44585CB00013B/639